A Thriving Mind

A practical guide to developing resilience and positivity in young children

EDITED BY:

DOUG STRYCHARCZYK

AND TONI MOLYNEUX

Copyright © 2023 Resilient Hedgehog
All rights reserved.
ISBN: 9798866045310

CONTENTS

	Acknowledgements	vii
	Introduction	1
1	**What is mental toughness and why is it relevant?** *Raising young people who can deal with the vagaries of life and see the opportunities when all seems dark.*	3
2	Why is my mental toughness or mental sensitivity significant in parenting?	17
3	We are nearly all normal	34
4	Dealing with children's attitudes	38
5	Fostering psychological safety and emotional well-being	49
6	Dealing with children's behaviour	68
7	Supporting the development of positive peer relationships	77
8	Understanding and supporting through trauma, adversity and loss	96
9	Self-regulation, co-regulation vs co-escalation (self-awareness)	105
10	Putting things into context	117
11	The importance of developing mental toughness	118
12	Cultivating mental toughness in children. Empowering strategies for parents	130
13	Developing mental toughness	140
14	A toolkit for developing mental toughness	148
15	Developing a child's mental toughness through books	173
16	Summary	181
	References	182
	About the Authors	183

INTRODUCTION

WHAT IS THE PURPOSE OF THIS BOOK?

This book seeks to support parents, teachers, mentors and coaches etc. in understanding and developing mental toughness in children aged 2-8 years.

It will do so through exploring different dimensions of parenting including dealing with children's attitudes, psychological safety and emotional well-being, behaviours, peer relationships, co-regulation and escalation as well as dealing with trauma, adversity and loss.

This book is driven by demand. In our core work we work with business leaders, and employees at all levels and of all types. The focus is generally on their performance and well-being at work (and in life). Very often they are also parents who recognise the value of developing resilience and positivity in their children to prepare them for the challenges of life. We are very commonly asked, "How can I do this with my children?"

This book responds to that call.

It also responds to a demand from more enlightened educators who commit to providing a more holistic education to those in their charge which prepares them for life after school and college. Again, this is responding vicariously to a demand from parents. This is what most also want from the world of education.

The book addresses the issues commonly reported by parents as being areas of concern or challenge in terms of understanding and supporting their children. Here we bring together the views of professionals to present how these areas of concern related to mental toughness as well as how understanding your mental toughness as a parent and your child's mental toughness can help.

This book also presents a variety of practical tools and development suggestions to support you in understanding and developing mental toughness and self-awareness for yourself and your child.

1 WHAT IS MENTAL TOUGHNESS AND WHY IS IT RELEVANT?

Raising children who can deal with the vagaries of life and see the opportunities when all seems dark.

Doug Strycharczyk

Mental toughness is an important concept. It has long been known to be important. 2,500 years ago, Plato described it as one of the four cardinal virtues. He used the term Fortitude which has been defined as "the inner strength to keep going for some higher end when everything seems very hard".

Those four cardinal virtues underpin other virtues and are often said to be where our values come from. The four virtues are:

- Justice (the idea of rights and commitment to defending these rights).
- Wisdom (self-awareness and learning from our experiences and others).
- Fortitude (courage – the strength to do what we need to do).
- Temperance (self-control and self-worth).

Arguably, mental toughness is relevant to at least two of the other virtues (Wisdom and Temperance). As adults, we value these qualities in ourselves. As parents, we aspire to see them develop in our children.

Mental Toughness is now the widely accepted term for the capability to continue when things seem hard. The term toughness is not used in a "macho" or aggressive sense though.

Nor is it only about carrying on.

Some people may try to carry on during challenging times but ultimately this will be detrimental to their well-being. Instead, mental toughness describes the attributes and skills to keep going when things are hard, whilst remaining well, and developing.

This can sometimes require behaviours that may seem inconsistent with the word "toughness", such as seeking support or advice.

Mental toughness embraces the twin elements of resilience and positivity.

Resilience in the sense that there will be setbacks and adversity in everyone's lives, and resilience enables us to recover from this.

Positivity, in the sense that even in adversity, there will often be opportunity and beneficial challenge. With the right mindset, we can see the opportunity as well as the threat and have the self-belief to grasp the opportunity. This is where growth comes from.

Other broadly equivalent terms often used to describe something similar include mindset, resilience, character and even grit and tenacity. Attitude is also a commonly used expression.

The good news for parents is that mental toughness, to a certain extent, is something that can be enhanced given the right environment and support. Therefore, there are things we can do to help our children develop the attributes that comprise mental toughness.

In 2002, Professor Peter Clough proposed what is now called the 4Cs model of mental toughness which began to create an understanding of the concept and, importantly, allowed people to use it for development.

Since then, collaboration between researchers and practitioners has enabled a deeper understanding by identifying eight factors that contribute to one's overall mental toughness.

This is extremely useful in understanding how we, and our children, respond mentally to what happens to us, and around us. We now know this is a fundamentally important aspect of our personality.

In turn, this helps us to better understand why we act the way we do in response to events. In other words, why we behave the way we do – the other important aspect of our personality.

Developing good and appropriate behaviours is a key goal in parenting.

There is now considerable independent academic evidence to support this concept together with an increasing body of case studies and projects which support the idea that this is a key concept in the development of people of all ages.

Amongst many things, the research shows that mental toughness is a factor in:

- **Attainment** – getting things done and doing what is important for you and others. In young people, this is relevant for exams and academic success.
- **Well-being** – managing the psychological consequences of life – anxiety, depression, stress and sleep.

- **Agility** - the capacity to readily respond to change, crisis, challenge and new circumstances, taking these in your stride.
- **Aspirations** - the positivity to believe in oneself that you can be the best version of yourself that you can be.

It is important to understand that the mental toughness concept is a continuum with mental toughness at one end and mental sensitivity at the other end. This is also true for the components of mental toughness which we are about to describe.

We all sit at different points on that continuum. These are not labels in the sense they indicate good or bad, strength or weakness. It is the case though, that, all things being equal, possessing a degree of mental toughness conveys an advantage in many useful settings.

It is also the case that, by creating self-awareness and development, the mentally sensitive can prosper and in the absence of these, the mentally tough can struggle.

Nurturing this aspect of our personality can benefit everyone.

What do we know about mental toughness?

Clough found that it had four elements – Control, Commitment, Challenge and Confidence. Each consists of two factors.

The first element, Control, describes in essence, the extent to which we believe we have sufficient control of ourselves, our lives and our circumstances to achieve what is important for us to achieve.

Some have that inner sense of "can do" – others do not. Two

people may be identical in abilities, skills etc. but, when asked to do something, one will hesitate before acting and may never act, while the other will leap forward and "give it a go". The difference is entirely in the mind.

One of the factors is **Life Control**. This describes the sense of self-worth – the extent to which a person believes in themselves and sees themselves as someone who can generally do what is needed. They see themselves as worthwhile individuals. They are often described as having a "can do" attitude.

Where there is a low level of Life Control, the individual will instinctively look for reasons why they cannot do what is asked of them. Although these may seem trivial to others, they can become valid (in their mind) reasons for not even trying.

The second factor is **Emotional Control**. In a sense, we cannot control our emotions. If we are unhappy, we are sad. If we are upset, we feel wretched.

However, it is not always helpful to reveal our emotions to others – especially in adulthood. Maintaining a degree of poise or apparent indifference helps us to deal with provocation, bullying and even accidental setbacks.

Similarly, not managing our emotions can mean that at times we will allow our emotions to significantly affect our actions and the decisions we make. Managing our emotions is likely to lead to better behaviours and decisions.

Again, some can deal more effectively with their emotion than others.

The second element, **Commitment,** describes the extent to which we understand what it is we need to do and are mentally prepared to make the effort to do it.

It is closely related to the behaviour known as conscientiousness.

Again, this element has two factors.

The first is **Goal Orientation**. This describes the extent to which an individual can visualise what is important for them and can picture what success might look like. It is about knowing their purpose. From this, they can derive goals. It should be a source of motivation for most.

Some can think in terms of goals and visualise the desired outcome. Others cannot and in many cases will not. For a child, it could be a tidy bedroom, tidying up after play or doing well enough in class or in play to be selected for the team.

The second factor is **Achievement Orientation**. This describes the mental approach towards making the effort to achieve those goals. Some will have that internal motivation, understanding what achievement looks and feels like and wanting that sufficiently to commit to making the effort. Even if it is not something the individual wants to do.

It is about attaining a sense of satisfaction that, despite everything, you made the effort and succeeded.

Some will find the idea of effort disagreeable in some way and will not commit to making that effort.

The elements of Control and Commitment broadly equate to what is described as Resilience. They help us to recover from adversity, they help us to survive when things become difficult.

The next two elements introduce positivity into the picture.

Challenge is the third element. This describes how we react mentally to dealing with challenges, new experiences, opportunities and unforeseen events (including crises) as well as how we respond to the experience. That is, do we learn from all that we experience?

It explains why some will see opportunity in a situation while others will tend to see the threat.

It is particularly significant for young people. For them, life will be a constant stream of transitions and new experiences – going to nursery, then to infant school then to junior school and so on. Joining clubs and meeting new people. The transition from a known "comfortable" setting to a new and potentially strange setting can be particularly challenging.

There are two factors here. **Risk Orientation** is one. This describes the extent to which we are open to trying something new or different and which, perhaps, carries a degree of risk being unknown.

Some will prefer to avoid any form of change or having to deal with any form of the unfamiliar. Others may be excited to see what a new situation or experience will bring.

Note that it is possible to be confident in one's abilities and still avoid situations where these abilities are useful.

The second factor is **Learning Orientation**. Sometimes described as the "beating heart" of the mental toughness concept, this describes the extent to which one reflects on all that happens to them and around them... and learns valuable lessons from that. Given that childhood and adolescence are one continuous learning journey this is an important quality.

Some will extract learning from all their experiences which helps to build their mental toughness across all factors. This is especially true of setbacks and failures. Others may not do this and can see some experiences as best ignored or forgotten.

This openness to learning can embrace a willingness to see learning as a useful way of making progress and improving oneself.

From a parent's perspective, it is worth understanding that whilst children do not always do what you tell them to do, they will however often copy what they see you do. Your behaviour matters.

This, of course, describes the nurture element of nature (genetic) and nurture explanations for the development of our personality.

Challenge thus begins to explain why some are optimistic about life.

The fourth element, **Confidence**, adds to that explanation. This describes self-belief – in our talent to be able to deal with whatever occurs and to take difficulty and opportunity in our stride. Two factors contribute to this element.

One factor is **Confidence in Abilities**. This describes the extent to which the child has self-belief in their abilities.

Some will have skills, knowledge etc. and will know this and that they can use these. Particularly knowing that they can deal with whatever comes their way.

Others can have excellent abilities but will still doubt that they have these abilities. In which case they may avoid using these abilities and may underperform, struggle without good reason or worry about their abilities.

Often seen in examination or test settings, perfectly able people hesitate to offer an answer because they are not certain that they have the necessary grasp of a subject when they do.

The final factor is **Interpersonal Confidence**. Some will readily engage with others, believing that they can influence others as much as others do them. They see the positives in connecting readily with other people. Their behaviour can be described as outgoing or gregarious.

On the other hand, some will avoid social interaction, lacking the confidence to engage with others and finding it difficult to be noticed. They will often be described as shy or reserved.

This is important in developing peer relationships. It is also significant in the extent to which young people are prepared to ask questions without feeling "stupid" or embarrassed in so doing.

A great deal of learning can be fed to a young person but asking questions to add to that learning or to clarify and understand what is being provided can be particularly important.

There are some things important to bear in mind here which apply to all of the elements and factors.

In the first place, the concept, its elements and factors have so far been described as if they are stand-alone factors. Each contributes to this important aspect of personality in its own way.

However, although these are independent to a significant extent, they can also combine to produce another valuable and important level of understanding.

For instance, if we look at Commitment, we can see several

combinations. It is possible to have a higher level of goal orientation and a low level of achievement orientation. This could mean that the individual knows what needs to be done, and wants to do it but cannot muster the effort to actually do it. That can have many consequences.

On the other hand, it is possible to have a lower level of goal orientation and a higher level of achievement orientation. This could now mean that the individual does not have a view of what they need to achieve and why but when presented with goals from elsewhere, they may gain a lot of satisfaction from doing what is required and completing tasks.

This kind of analysis is applied to all four elements. It applies equally to factors between elements.

An individual who has a high level of life control, but a low level of risk orientation will be different to an individual with a low level of life control and a high level of risk orientation.

The former will have a sense of "can do" but will prefer to operate in familiar surroundings. The latter will be curious about exploring new settings and situations but may lack the sense of self-worth to actually go there.

We often represent the mental toughness concept in the form of a "pizza" image where each factor can be seen in its place. It is easier to consider the connections between factors too.

Why is Mental Toughness important for my approach to life?

What I learn at school

- How to add, multiply and subtract
- How to read and write
- Lots of information about the world - history, geography, science, languages etc.

All very useful and important. It is part of what I need to be the best that I can be.

A very big part of the rest is about my attitude...

What I also need to learn

Why making an effort and focusing on my goals is important.

Why goals and targets are valuable.

To be open to new ideas and to see opportunity.

To learn from all that happens especially my mistakes.

To manage my emotions and not allow my emotions to manage me.

To have faith in me that I can "do it!"

To believe in my abilities and to use them.

To engage with others to learn and show what I can do.

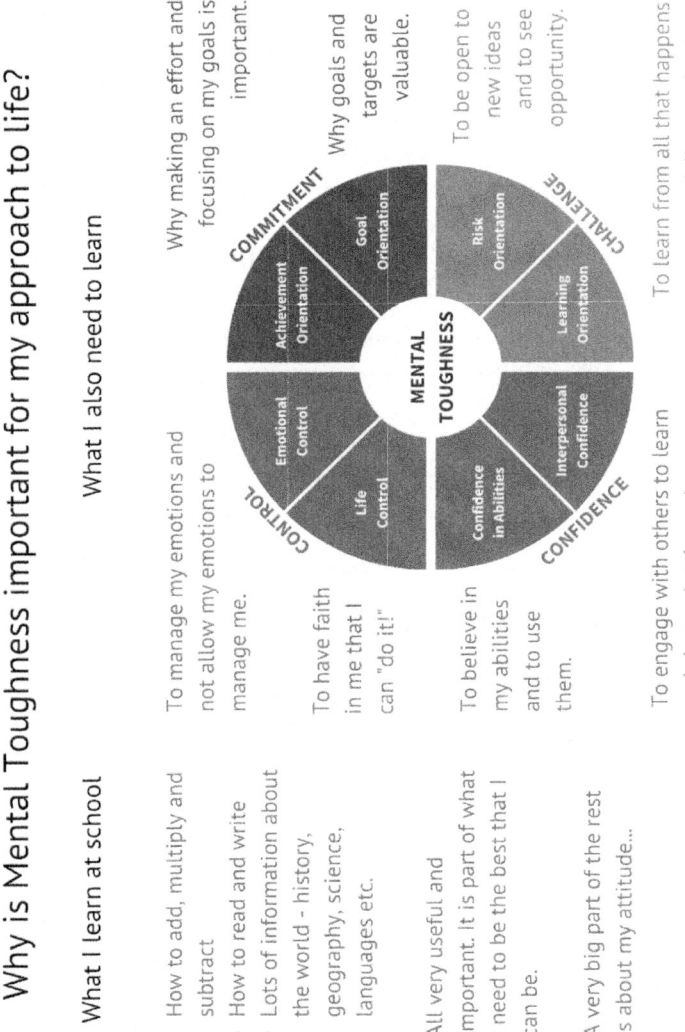

Fig. 1: *Mental Toughness and my approach to life*

Secondly, when looking at children, it will often be the case that most will have several areas where they may need some form of development activity.

So, for any child, some or even all of these factors are influencing how they approach what happens in their lives and how they behave. It is important to approach developing young children with an open mind. There will rarely be one issue to consider and one perfect solution.

We know that it is possible to learn how to be more mentally tough or to learn how to cope effectively with areas of mental sensitivity. Most of this is learned through experiential learning as we go through life.

As with any form of learning, the better the guidance, the better the learning. Parents, guardians, carers and teachers have a key role here in supporting young children to learn from their experiences.

In general, most adults learn or have sufficient mental toughness to deal with most setbacks, challenges and opportunities. They may not deal with all, but they have enough to survive and will sometimes thrive.

Some, with a high level of mental toughness, can find they breeze through life. A small number are described as mentally sensitive (i.e., have a low level of mental toughness). They feel every bump on the road through life and can struggle to cope with these.

The reassuring news is that, with self-awareness, the mentally sensitive can lead a fulfilling life – but this does require self-awareness, reflection and learning.

Having read about the importance of mental toughness and

elements of mental toughness above, you may now be asking yourself questions like "Is my child mentally tough?".

Some indicators of the 4Cs might be observed in children. For example, a child who sets goals to complete their homework (e.g., says they will answer 5 questions today and then 5 questions tomorrow) may be demonstrating commitment, and a child who makes friends easily and is happy to speak in front of others could be displaying confidence.

However, in the context of parenting, we need to understand that young children are at the start of their journey through life. Most are likely to be predominantly mentally sensitive. They have not yet learned to adopt the kind of mental responses that enable them to do more than survive.

Our general expectation should be that they are not like me (an adult), and I need to understand.

- Who they are,
- Why they do not respond the way I do and,

from that, begin the process of helping them to respond better.

This process might involve providing the right environment and support to cultivate the development of mental toughness, allowing a child to face new and potentially difficult tasks so that they can learn through experiential learning, and encouraging a child to reflect upon and become self-aware about the elements of mental toughness.

A useful way of beginning discussions about the elements of mental toughness may be through stories. For young people, storytelling is a useful way of learning.

As many parents will know, even a model child can resist being told what to do by their parents. Illustrate the same behaviour or attitude in a story about a third party (human or fictional) and the child can identify with that character and learn that behaviour. The Resilient Hedgehog books as described in Chapter 15, are very much created to achieve this effect.

We will look at developing children's mental toughness more in later chapters. Before this being self-aware about our own mental toughness as parents is equally important. We look at this in the next chapter.

2 WHY IS MENTAL TOUGHNESS OR MENTAL SENSITIVITY IMPORTANT IN PARENTING?

Doug Strycharczyk

Mental toughness is important for parenting in at least two ways.

Firstly, it is important for us as parents in terms of allowing us to navigate the many challenges that parenthood presents. There are times when parenting can be joyous and rewarding, but other times when it can be difficult and exhausting, therefore requiring us to be mentally tough.

Secondly, mental toughness is important because it influences how we behave as parents, and we know that parenting behaviours have an important influence on childhood development. Thus, through our own mental toughness, we have the potential to influence the well-being, aspirations, agility, and attainment of our children.

When we examine mental toughness, we learn that the origin of some of our mental toughness is genetic and some is the product of our experiences and how they shape us.

In our work with adults in business, education, etc., we see that the most important experiential influences often come from those who lead, manage and guide people. Peers influence us too. Making a difference usually means starting with those who influence us.

It is the same for young people. Before school, the most important influences are parents, relatives or guardians.

Once they enter the education system, teachers and peers

become, along with parents, a major influence.

And again, peers are also relevant. We know from research that there is a relationship between a young person's level of mental toughness and the extent to which they build peer relationships. It is also often the case that young people will learn from their peers as much as they do from other influences.

This means that being self-aware about our own mental toughness and mental sensitivity as parents and teachers is important. It influences our own behaviour which influences others. Just as importantly it influences the way we respond to others – to children.

It can be easy to forget children are children. They are not small adults.

When they show behaviours and emotional responses which we would prefer they did not show, we can forget they are young, and we can judge them as if they are adults.

Self-awareness about our mental approach to others is difficult. It is understanding what we think when we interact with a child.

By far the most effective way of doing this is to complete the MTQPlus questionnaire and consider what the report indicates. Especially when supported by feedback and exploration from a trained user of the measure. Both incur a cost.

The purpose of this chapter is to provide insight into why self-awareness is so important, especially with this application.

We will do this by looking at each factor and exploring how someone who is mentally tough or mentally sensitive might respond to others, particularly children.

Amongst other things, we will refer to some dimensions of parenting. Scientists agree that there are at least two broad dimensions of parenting.

The first of these is parental support, sometimes referred to as responsiveness. This describes involvement, emotional availability, and warmth, and is related to positive developmental outcomes in children.

The second dimension is parental control, sometimes called demandingness. An appropriate amount of control is thought to be important for child development, whereas insufficient or excessive control (particularly psychological control) has been linked to more negative outcomes.

Sometimes these parenting dimensions have been considered together in the form of parenting styles, for example, high parental support and high parental control have been referred to as authoritative parenting, which is thought to be the most successful style.

We do not intend to look in detail at these parenting styles, but rather to provide an insight into how mental toughness may impact supportive or controlling behaviours. It is important to note though, that more research is needed to fully understand the role of mental toughness in parenting.

The approach we will take is a deliberate oversimplification. We will consider high and low levels of each component of mental toughness, but each of the factors is a continuum and most people will have a level of mental toughness or mental sensitivity at some point between the extremes.

Starting with **Life Control**.

Life Control	I think I am worthwhile - I will "give most things a go".
Emotional Control	I can manage my emotions and make good decisions.

Someone with a high level of life control will typically have a strong sense of self-worth. For them not much is impossible. They will normally "have a go" when asked to do something that others might hesitate to do.

When managing several things, they can be adept at prioritising and planning and will generally be able to manage several tasks at a time.

A consequence for them can be that they are over-ambitious and apply that to others. They can be open to doing things that others are not ready to do and may not always appreciate the extent of this.

If attempting to do more than one thing at a time with a child, they can fail to understand why the child is confused.

A result can be frustration and impatience with its inevitable consequences.

For those with high levels of life control, it is also important not to try to exert too much control over the lives of children. Excessive control can be detrimental if this is at the cost of parental support.

As children grow and develop, they need to practice autonomy, making their own choices and making their own mistakes. Using supportive behaviours, like discussing actions and their consequences, is likely to be more helpful than using controlling behaviours such as punishing children if they break the rules.

In contrast, those with lower levels of life control will generally feel they do not have sufficient control to achieve what they need. They can feel that things happen to them and that their children's behaviours are out of their control. They might accept a child's responses and feel unable to change or influence them. Children will often "test" adults.

In these situations, a mentally sensitive parent might feel they are losing what control they have and allow their child to have their way. They can doubt their worth as parents, and this may lead to less supportive parenting. A result can be a sense of helplessness – giving up on the challenge of being a parent.

Emotional Control describes another aspect of control.

Life Control	I think I am worthwhile – I will "give most things a go".
Emotional Control	I can manage my emotions and make good decisions.

Generally, we cannot control what we feel when something happens. What we should be able to control is the extent to which we manage our mental responses to these emotions. This has some applications in parenting.

If we are mentally sensitive in terms of emotional control, we can be prone to revealing our emotional state to others. A stubborn child can make us angry, frustrated, sad, etc. Any number of emotions. We know that it is not always helpful to reveal our emotional state to others.

In the first place, the shown behaviour can role model that behaviour for a child. When parents display more negative emotions such as anger, then children also display these emotions.

It is also probable that decisions made to deal with a situation might be shaped by a parent's emotions. Anger, frustration, annoyance, etc. are rarely good ingredients in decision-making.

These kinds of emotions are more likely to lead to controlling parenting behaviours, such as disapproval and punishment, perhaps at the cost of supportive behaviours.

Of course, revealing something of our emotional state can be important in social settings. It can be useful to reveal at times that we are happy, sad, upset, etc. Children need to understand something of the potential consequences of their behaviours.

The more mentally tough parents in this respect can be particularly good at controlling what they reveal, sometimes to the point of being impassive irrespective of what happens. This too can give rise to issues. If a child cannot read their parents, then they may not learn how to recognise whether they have pleased or disappointed their parents and why that may be.

To return briefly to role modelling, sometimes good emotional control in the long term comes from using learned strategies (for example relaxation, deep breathing, or mindfulness). Just as our displays of emotion can model things for our children, using helpful strategies can also model approaches that children may find useful in the future.

Moving on to **Goal Orientation**.

Goal Orientation	I have self-belief in my abilities to deal with things.
Achievement Orientation	I am prepared to work hard & do what it takes to succeed.

Here we are looking at the extent to which a parent can visualise what they would like to achieve with their children – behaviours, attitudes, interests etc.

The more mentally sensitive the less clear this picture can be. A degree of clarity enables us to articulate what we are looking for and to direct ourselves towards that.

A lack of clarity can mean we say one thing and then another which can confuse a child. And it is harder to remain focused on what is important if it is fuzzy. This can lead to inconsistent parenting, such as sometimes using controlling behaviours and other times not.

For example, if a child misbehaves one day a parent might take away the child's privileges, but on another day the parent might not react to the same behaviour. This sort of parenting is confusing for a child.

Those who are very goal-orientated can set goals for everything, restricting the freedom of others to contribute or shape their own goals. The consequences of this may be like those of high life control that were discussed earlier.

Children need to learn to make their own choices and deal with the consequences. Goal orientation also does not necessarily mean that these goals are attainable. We can seem to demand too much of others at times, although often just driven by wanting our children to be healthy, liked, and successful.

We are most motivated to work towards achieving the goals that we set for ourselves though, so setting goals for our children is less likely to influence our children than if they set goals for themselves.

Achievement Orientation describes whether you are prepared mentally to make the effort to do what you need or "what is good for you".

Goal Orientation	I have self-belief in my abilities to deal with things.
Achievement Orientation	I am prepared to work hard & do what it takes to succeed.

Young children will often not yet be at the stage where they can visualise what completing a task feels like. They may not yet understand the sense of satisfaction that doing a good job brings. They will see the effort before they see the outcome and may be put off by that.

Interestingly most parents were like that at one time... but may have forgotten this. Not everyone had a tidy bedroom or cleared their toys when finished playing with them or helped clear up the dinner table.

An achievement-orientated parent can be intolerant of those who will not make even a small effort. They can make demands from their children that may not be realistic. Importantly they may not understand why their children do not respond as expected. Frustration can lead to more demanding parenting, which if at the cost of supportive parenting can be detrimental.

Another possible response is that the conscientious parent may give up supporting the child's development and begin to do what the child should do in the belief they are setting an example. They are setting an example, but if not carefully managed, the example they are setting is that someone else will make the effort to sort things out; what Professor Seligman called learned helplessness.

Low levels of achievement orientation can also be problematic for parents. Parents who have a lower level of achievement orientation are less inclined to make effort themselves, including effort directed towards their children's development. They may give up when the going gets tough. They may not complete important tasks. They may leave things unfinished. This is likely to mean less supportive and less involved parenting.

The upshot can be that they become a role model for an approach that underachieves.

The factors described thus far are in a sense operational factors. They are describing what a parent might do, and do better, to be effective.

The next factors embrace this to a degree, but they can also bring an element of positivity and optimism to the picture.

The first of these is **Risk Orientation**.

Risk Orientation	I see opportunity when exposed to new situations.
Learning Orientation	I think about all that happens to me and learn from that.

Parenting for many is a new experience and even when repeated it is rarely the same each time. Each child can be quite different in terms of their personality.

Risk orientation describes the extent to which a person is open to new experiences, new situations, new people, etc. Openness means being prepared to have to do things you might not have done or seen before.

Those with lower levels of risk orientation might have a predetermined or fixed idea of what the parenting experience is and how, for instance, a child should behave. This is recognised somehow as the "norm".

This is not what parenting is like. It is a continuous exposure to new situations as a child grows and develops. If there is a low level of risk orientation then issues and occurrences can arise leading to frustration, annoyance, and feelings of inadequacy because you feel you cannot cope. The avoidance of risk or challenge may translate into avoidance of effortful disciplinary practices, and more reliance on strategies to control children's behaviour. Avoiding difficult situations could also result in shying away from addressing child misbehaviour altogether, which is of course not good for children.

Like many things in life, what you do not expect will often happen. The challenge is to be agile and flexible enough to be able to recognise that and take it in your stride.

Having too high a degree of risk orientation also has its potential downsides. You can be so open to new experiences etc. that you may not pay sufficient attention to things like structure and the development of rules or norms that are important for social interaction. "Anything goes" is not always the best lesson a child can learn.

A high degree of risk orientation could also mean parents trying new approaches or strategies with their children too often, leading to inconsistent parenting, which can be confusing for children.

Learning Orientation often sits alongside risk orientation.

Risk Orientation	I see opportunity when exposed to new situations.
Learning Orientation	I think about all that happens to me and learn from that.

It is one thing to push boundaries and try new things, it is another to assess them and to learn from those experiences. It is in the nature of trying new ideas and approaches with a child that some or many may not work well or at all.

Those with a degree of learning orientation are typically those who are most reflective. They consider what they do and its consequences. They extract the learning from that and build it into the routines and approaches they adopt as part of their parenting armoury in the comparatively secure knowledge that this has worked... and is likely like to work again.

This helps with avoiding repeating mistakes as well as repeatedly doing something that patently does not work.

Some parents can take this too far and continuously reflect, learn, and adjust what they do without settling on a course of action that might otherwise work well enough. Too much change, or inconsistent parenting, can unsettle children and frustrate parents.

Those with a low level of learning orientation are likely to not think too much about what happens when they interact with or do things with their children. This can mean that they do not learn what works and what does not, and they do not then learn how to improve or whether they need to change it.

This can be the source of inadequacy – "I keep trying but it doesn't seem to work, I am a failure" – as well as frustration "I keep repeating what I have been shown and I am now getting annoyed when it doesn't work".

Finally, we come to self-belief – known better as confidence. Two aspects can be important here.

The first is **Confidence in our Abilities** as a parent.

Confidence in Abilities	I have self-belief in my abilities to deal with things.
Interpersonal Confidence	I am happy to engage with and to influence others.

The emphasis here is on confidence more so than on abilities. We all have abilities in dealing with people – some can be transferable from other settings. If we have engaged with others as adults, we will have some experience in dealing with a range of personalities and behaviours.

Often parenting for us happens at the same time as parenting happens for our peers. We see what they do. We may attend basic classes with peers and share learning experiences.

The issue here is that those who have a high degree of confidence in their abilities are more likely to use them or try to use them. Confidence in parenting, therefore, promotes adaptive parenting skills such as responsiveness and active and direct parenting interactions.

Such parents are also more often confident about acquiring new skills and abilities which they will use. Self-belief has also been related to effort and persistence, which are often necessary for parenting when we are confronted with obstacles or challenges.

Apart from being more effective as a parent, creating an environment where confidence is a recognisable component can also be good for a child's development.

Of course, there are potential downsides to having a great degree of confidence about one's abilities as a parent. You might think you know it all and you can do it all. That is unlikely and can be problematic – as a parent you might just try to do things that are truly beyond your capability.

Those with a low degree of confidence in their abilities are likely to shy away from doing things with their children that are important for their development simply because they do not think they can do it. They could have learned how to do it, but they doubt themselves and, sometimes, are put off because they think others can do it better.

A lack of confidence can result in feelings of helplessness in the parenting role, poorer parent well-being, and more use of either passive parenting or coercive discipline. This can increase the risk of poor child behaviour.

In short, more confidence in abilities is related to an ability to foster a healthy and supportive childrearing environment.

The other dimension is **Interpersonal Confidence.**

Confidence in Abilities	I have self-belief in my abilities to deal with things.
Interpersonal Confidence	I am happy to engage with and to influence others.

This reflects the extent to which, as a parent, you are mentally prepared to engage with a child and the extent to which you feel you can influence them.

Given that developing social skills in a child is one of the most valuable things you can do to prepare them for adulthood this factor has some considerable significance. Research shows that engaging children from age three in conversation is a major contributor to those social skills.

Interpersonal confidence is also important in supporting children to develop many of the qualities we describe above.

Those with a good degree of interpersonal confidence are likely to build good relationships with their children. Engagement will be strong – explaining what a parent expects from their children, providing feedback and guidance and listening to the child to understand their needs. This is supportive parenting.

It is also possible to apply too much interpersonal confidence. Without self-awareness, it is possible to dominate exchanges, not listen enough and be so dominant that the child learns not to interrupt or contribute. In other words, parents can be controlling. This hampers development.

Some parents will inevitably have lower levels of interpersonal confidence. They are much less comfortable engaging with children often keeping interaction to a minimum. For instance, when reading stories to children they may simply read the story without exploring the nuances that engage with and can intrigue, a child.

In some instances, the child may dominate the parent. Displaying emotions, being persistently stubborn and shouting are examples of approaches that children can use to influence their parents more than their parents will them.

We can summarise the role of mental toughness in parenting in the figure below.

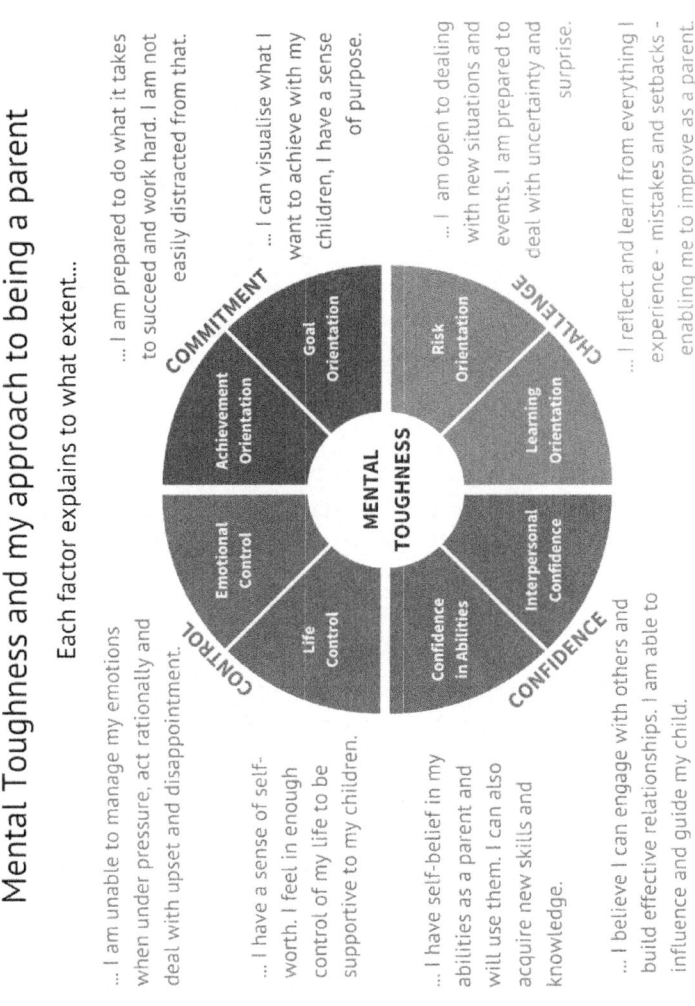

Fig. 2: *Mental Toughness and my approach to parenting*

The purpose of this chapter is to reinforce the idea that parenting is a multifaceted experience and that one of the most important dimensions is the personality and mental toughness of the parents.

The fact is that parents should, with teachers, be the dominant influence on a child's development.

To summarise how mental toughness relates to parenting, having very high or very low levels of each dimension of mental toughness has the potential to be problematic. Most of us, however, have a level of mental toughness which is somewhere between these extremes. Reflection upon our mental toughness and how this might influence parenting is especially important though.

As with any development activity, we do need to understand our children and how they respond mentally to what happens to them and around them so that they can develop better responses to those events – especially in adulthood.

However, our own personality and mental toughness are not separate from this. Our own mental approaches to the challenges, opportunities and stressors inherent in being a parent are just as important.

Developing a child starts with understanding and developing yourself. Realistic self-awareness is essential.

The chapters illustrate, albeit briefly, the range of responses we can adopt and highlight some of the many consequences of those mental responses. This may also be useful and valuable in another sense.

As parents, we will often co-parent and sometimes liaise with others such as teachers, carers, etc. Those relationships, crucially important, can work well or be a source of problems. The explanation for this can often be found in the difference in mental toughness.

A parent who has a significantly lower level of interpersonal confidence than their partner might feel disengaged and shout out from contributing as a parent.

Differences in risk orientation may lead to disagreements about the kinds of experiences the child might be exposed to. And so on.

It is also the case that our levels of mental toughness do not sit in isolation. They generally interplay with other factors influencing our behaviour – these include biases, interests, levels of education, skills and knowledge, levels of support etc.

They too can contribute to the way we are perceived by others and how accessible we are to other sources of support, guidance etc. when parenting.

Self-awareness matters a great deal when seeking to be the best parent that you can be.

3 WE ARE NEARLY ALL NORMAL

Dorien van 't Ende and Toni Molyneux

As a parent, especially a first-time parent, it's very easy to worry about your child and your parenting abilities. The smallest change in their physical health, their mental well-being or their behaviour can keep you awake at night. You may have found yourself scouring the internet for answers and it may have led to even more questions and worries than answers. Everyone has their opinions and advice on how to raise a child and what to expect of your child. There's a lot of information about children hitting milestones and certain behaviours to expect at certain ages. At the same time, this information comes with a sidenote that all children develop at their own pace. So, you're left wondering 'Is what my child is doing normal?', or 'Am I doing a good enough job?'.

We didn't need to do much digging to find out that all parents struggle with certain behaviours at a certain point in their parenting career. Some parents may struggle more than others – whether it be because of their own or their child's resilience and mental toughness, because their child develops at a different pace than what is considered to be the norm, or simply not knowing what to expect and how to deal with particular situations. It may at times feel like you're the only one that is dealing with certain issues. A quick look at your friends' seemingly perfect children on social media will probably only add to the stress. However, it turns out that there are some very common themes. These themes have been identified and will be addressed in this book.

So, the answers to the above questions are most likely 'Yes. Yes, your child is normal and, yes, you are doing a good enough job.' But what is normal? And, more specifically, what is normal from a mental toughness perspective? In life, most things are distributed normally. This includes one's qualities and abilities. Mental Toughness appears to be distributed in the same pattern. Someone's mental toughness is explored through normative research, which means that the results of an individual's test are compared to a larger group. The results of this can be visualised in a bell curve shown below (AQR International, 2023).

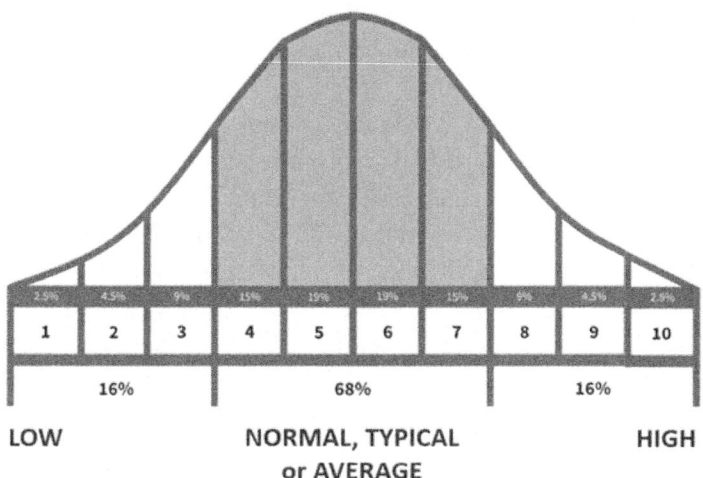

Fig. 3: *Normal distribution*

The scale is divided into 10 equal parts or stens. A sten (standard ten) shows a person's approximate position with respect to the values and other people in the population. The majority of the population, 68%, fall within the 4 to 7 range, which is considered to be normal.

This means that individuals in this range, overall, have a reasonable level of mental toughness. They may struggle at times, but in general, they go through life comfortably. For example, if you think of your own life, you may find some examples of where you and/or your child excel and somewhere you struggle.

For example, your child may be good at setting a goal, like tidying their room or finishing homework before a certain time (goal orientation), but they may find it difficult to actually get the job done (achievement orientation). They may need more help and encouragement to achieve their goal, but with guidance, they can get there. And you as a parent may feel very confident in getting your child to achieve these goals (confidence in abilities), but you might sometimes get upset or angry when you feel like your child isn't listening to you (emotional control).

But what if you fall outside of the normal range? As mentioned in Chapter 2, this isn't good or bad. There is no right or wrong when it comes to being mentally sensitive, mentally tough, or somewhere in the middle. Being mentally tough is not a guarantee for an easy life. Vice versa, being mentally sensitive doesn't mean your whole life will be a struggle. With proper guidance and development, mentally sensitive could prosper, and without, mentally tough could fail. Everyone on the spectrum is needed: artists tend to be more sensitive, and managers tougher.

There are advantages and disadvantages for all points across the scale. Therefore, whether you are mentally tough, mentally sensitive, somewhere in between or a combination of both, there are strengths and limitations.

The key to Mental Toughness is self-awareness. It is about understanding your strengths and limitations and what implications that has for your circumstances. What is considered to be a limitation for one person may be a strength for another in different circumstances.

So, one way or another, we are nearly all normal. We are all excellent at some things and not so great at others. The same goes for our children. With self-awareness, we can make sure we are the version of ourselves that we want to be and guide children to become positive, resilient and mentally tough.

4 DEALING WITH CHILDREN'S ATTITUDES

Anna Golawski

This chapter is going to have a look at the attitudes of children and how they relate to mental toughness components. It will also have a look at what we can do to manage and mitigate unwanted attitudes that children may display, and how we can manage our own emotions and well-being to be effective.

Dealing with young children's attitudes can be a challenging task for any parent or caregiver. Children are still in the process of developing their personalities, and as a result, they often exhibit various attitudes that can range from positive to negative. Some children may be naturally curious and creative, while others may be more defiant and rebellious. Regardless of the attitude, it is essential to deal with children in a way that is both effective and positive.

With patience, consistency, and positive reinforcement, parents and caregivers can help children develop positive attitudes and behaviours that will serve them well throughout their lives.

Discipline and Sanctions

Discipline is an important aspect of parenting, and it involves setting boundaries and rules for children to follow. Discipline helps children learn to control their behaviour and make responsible choices. It is essential to set clear expectations for children and establish consequences for their actions.

When it comes to discipline, parents should avoid using physical punishment or shaming as it can have negative effects on a child's self-esteem and mental health. Instead, parents should focus on positive reinforcement and discipline that promotes self-esteem, responsibility, and respect.

One effective way to discipline young children is through time-outs. Time-outs involve placing the child in a designated area where they can calm down and reflect on their behaviour. Time-outs are an effective way to help children understand that their behaviour has consequences without being overly harsh.

Sanctions are also an important aspect of discipline. Parents should establish clear sanctions for specific behaviours, such as hitting or disrespecting others. The sanctions should be age-appropriate and relevant to the behaviour. For example, if a child hits another child, a sanction might be removing the toy they were playing with at the time. Sanctions should also be consistently enforced to reinforce the importance of following rules.

Rewards and Positive Reinforcement

Rewards and positive reinforcement are an essential part of parenting young children. Children respond well to positive feedback, and rewards can help reinforce positive behaviour. Rewards can be as simple as a sticker chart or a small treat. They should be age-appropriate and relevant to the behaviour.

It is essential to use rewards and positive reinforcement in conjunction with discipline. Parents should reinforce positive behaviour and encourage children to make responsible choices. For example, if a child helps clean up their toys without being asked, they might receive a small treat or extra playtime.

Building Trust

Building trust is an essential aspect of parenting young children. Children who feel that they can trust their parents are more likely to be open and honest about their feelings and actions. Trust is built through consistent and positive interactions with children.

Parents should make an effort to spend quality time with their children regularly. This time can be spent playing games, reading books, or simply talking. It is essential to be present and engaged during this time and avoid distractions such as phones or televisions.

Another way to build trust is to listen to children's feelings and concerns. Children need to feel that their opinions are valued and heard. Parents should make an effort to listen actively and empathize with their children's feelings.

Creativity and Curiosity

Young children are naturally curious and creative, and parents should encourage this behaviour. Creativity and curiosity promote problem-solving skills and encourage children to explore the world around them. Parents can encourage creativity and curiosity by providing opportunities for children to engage in imaginative play, explore nature, or try new activities.

It is important to allow children to make their own choices and decisions. This encourages independence and self-esteem. For example, if a child wants to try a new activity, such as painting, parents should provide the materials and allow the child to experiment with the activity.

Mental Toughness and Attitudes of Children

Let's have a look at how this relates to mental toughness in young children and their attitudes.

As we have seen in earlier chapters there are 4 main components of Mental Toughness: Control, Commitment, Confidence and Challenge.

The **control** component of mental toughness refers to the ability to control one's thoughts, emotions, and behaviours in response to different situations. This aspect of mental toughness can positively influence children's attitudes in several ways.

Firstly, children who are high in the control component of mental toughness tend to have a greater sense of self-efficacy and control over their lives. They are more likely to believe that they can influence the outcomes of their actions and take responsibility for their choices, which can lead to a more positive attitude towards themselves and their abilities.

Secondly, children who are high in the control component of mental toughness tend to be more self-disciplined and goal-oriented. They are better able to delay gratification and resist temptations, which can lead to a more positive attitude towards the pursuit of long-term goals and personal growth.

Thirdly, children who are high in the control component of mental toughness tend to be more adaptable and flexible in response to changing circumstances. They are less likely to become overwhelmed by stress or anxiety and can maintain a more positive attitude towards uncertainty and ambiguity

However, it's important to note that too much control can also have negative effects on children's attitudes and behaviours. (Also see the chapter on behaviour). For instance, overly self-controlled children may become perfectionistic, overly critical of themselves or others, or may have difficulty relaxing or enjoying life. Therefore, it's important to encourage a balanced approach to mental toughness that promotes self-control while also allowing for flexibility, adaptability, and emotional expression.

The **commitment** component of mental toughness refers to the ability to set goals and maintain focus and motivation towards achieving those goals, even in the face of obstacles or setbacks. This aspect of mental toughness can positively influence children's attitudes in several ways.

Firstly, children who are high in the commitment component of mental toughness tend to have a more positive attitude towards their abilities and potential. They are more likely to set challenging goals for themselves and believe that they can achieve them, which can lead to a greater sense of confidence and self-efficacy.

Secondly, children who are high in the commitment component of mental toughness tend to have a stronger sense of purpose and direction in their lives. They are more likely to prioritise their goals and values, which can lead to a greater sense of meaning and fulfilment.

Thirdly, children who are high in the commitment component of mental toughness tend to be more resilient in the face of setbacks or failures. They are more likely to view obstacles as opportunities for growth and learning, which can lead to a more positive attitude towards challenges and setbacks.

However, it's important to note that too much commitment can also have negative effects on children's attitudes. For instance, children who are overly committed may become overly fixated on their goals, leading to a lack of balance in their lives and may miss out, or opt out of social or sporting activities. They may also become overly critical of themselves or others if they do not achieve their goals, leading to a negative attitude towards failure. Therefore, it's important to encourage a balanced approach that promotes commitment while also allowing for flexibility, adaptability, and self-care, including downtime.

The **confidence** component of mental toughness refers to the ability to believe in oneself and one's abilities, even in the face of uncertainty or adversity. This aspect of mental toughness can positively influence children's attitudes in several ways.

Firstly, children who are high in the confidence component of mental toughness tend to have a more positive attitude towards their abilities and potential. They are more likely to take on new challenges and opportunities, which can lead to a greater sense of accomplishment and satisfaction.

Secondly, children who are high in the confidence component of mental toughness tend to have a greater sense of self-worth and self-esteem. They are less likely to be influenced by negative feedback or criticism from others, which can lead to a more positive attitude towards themselves and their relationships.

Thirdly, children who are high in the confidence component of mental toughness tend to have a more positive attitude towards risk-taking and innovation. They are more likely to take calculated risks and try new things, which can lead to greater creativity and innovation.

However, it's important to note that too much confidence can also have negative effects on children's attitudes. For instance, overly confident children may become complacent or overestimate their abilities, leading to a lack of effort or preparation. They may also become overly critical of others or dismissive of feedback, leading to a negative attitude towards collaboration and teamwork. Therefore, it's important to encourage a balanced approach to mental toughness that promotes confidence while also allowing for humility, openness to feedback, and collaboration with others.

The **challenge** component of mental toughness refers to the ability to embrace and thrive in the face of difficult or uncertain situations. This aspect of mental toughness can positively influence children's attitudes in several ways.

Firstly, children who are high in the challenge component of mental toughness tend to have a more positive attitude towards difficult or uncertain situations. They are more likely to see challenges as opportunities for growth and learning, which can lead to greater resilience and adaptability.

Secondly, children who are high in the challenge component of mental toughness tend to have a greater sense of curiosity and creativity. They are more likely to explore new ideas and approaches, which can lead to greater innovation and problem-solving. Thirdly, children who are high in the challenge component of mental toughness tend to have a more positive attitude towards risk-taking and uncertainty. They are more likely to take calculated risks and try new things, which can lead to greater confidence and self-efficacy.

However, it's important to note that too much focus on challenges can also have negative effects on children's attitudes. For instance, children who are overly focused on challenges may become overwhelmed or stressed, leading to a negative attitude towards difficult or uncertain situations. They may also become overly competitive or perfectionistic, leading to a negative attitude towards themselves or others. Therefore, it's important to encourage a balanced approach to mental toughness that promotes a healthy challenge mindset while also allowing for self-care, stress management, and collaboration with others.

Preventing arguments escalating

Preventing arguments between parents and children can be a difficult task, especially when the child is exhibiting unwanted or undesirable attitudes. However, by using the right approach and communication techniques, parents can prevent arguments and foster a positive relationship with their children.

Acknowledge their feelings – When a child exhibits a

negative attitude, it is important to acknowledge their feelings and let them know that you understand where they are coming from. For example, if your child is angry about having to do their homework, you can acknowledge their frustration and offer to help them with the task. By acknowledging their feelings, you show them that you care about their concerns, and they are more likely to respond positively.

Communicate effectively - Effective communication is key to preventing arguments between parents and children. When you communicate with your child, it is important to listen actively, ask open-ended questions, and use a calm tone of voice. Avoid using negative language or threatening behaviour, as this can escalate the situation and lead to arguments.

Set clear boundaries and expectations – Setting clear boundaries and expectations is an important part of preventing arguments with children. When children know what is expected of them, they are less likely to act out and exhibit negative attitudes. Make sure to communicate your expectations clearly and follow through with consequences when necessary.

Use positive reinforcement – it's a powerful and effective tool for promoting positive behaviour in children. When your child exhibits a positive attitude or behaviour, make sure to praise and reward them. This can be as simple as saying "good job" or offering a small treat. By using positive reinforcement, you create a positive association with good behaviour, which can motivate your child to continue exhibiting positive attitudes.

Take a break – if you feel like an argument is imminent, it is important to take a break and remove yourself from the situation. This can help you calm down and prevent the argument from escalating. Encourage your child to take a break as well, and revisit the issue when you are both feeling calmer and more rational.

Humour can be a great way to diffuse tension and prevent arguments with children. When your child is exhibiting a negative attitude, try using humour to lighten the mood. This can be as simple as making a silly face or telling a joke. By using humour, you show your child that you are not taking their negative attitude personally, and you can help them see the situation in a more positive light.

Seek professional help if you are having difficulty preventing arguments with your child, it may be time to seek professional help. A counsellor or therapist can help you develop effective communication techniques and strategies for managing your child's behaviour. They can also provide support and guidance as you work to improve your relationship with your child.

In conclusion, preventing arguments between parents and children requires patience, communication, and a positive attitude. By acknowledging your child's feelings, communicating effectively, setting clear boundaries and expectations, using positive reinforcement, taking breaks, using humour, and seeking professional help when necessary, you can prevent arguments and foster a positive relationship with your child. Remember, raising a child is a journey, and it takes time, effort, and dedication to build a strong and positive relationship.

Keeping calm as a parent

Dealing with young children can be a challenging task, especially when they are being difficult. As a parent, it is essential to remain calm and composed during these situations to prevent the situation from escalating. Here are some tips on how to keep calm as a parent when dealing with young children.

Take a deep breath - When you feel yourself becoming frustrated or angry, take a deep breath and count to ten. This can help you calm down and regain your composure. You can also try some deep breathing exercises to help you relax and reduce stress.

Remind yourself of your child's age and development - It is important to remember that young children are still developing their emotional and social skills. When your child is being difficult, remind yourself of their age and stage of development. This can help you have more patience and understanding of their behaviour.

Use positive self-talk - Positive self-talk can be a powerful tool for keeping calm as a parent. When you feel yourself becoming frustrated, try saying positive affirmations to yourself, such as "I can handle this," or "I am a patient and loving parent." This can help you stay calm and confident in your parenting abilities.

Take a break - If you feel yourself becoming overwhelmed or stressed, take a break and remove yourself from the situation. You can take a few minutes to do something calming or enjoyable, such as reading a book or listening to music. This can help you relax and refocus your energy.

Practice mindfulness - Mindfulness is the practice of being present in the moment and fully aware of your thoughts and feelings. Practising mindfulness can help you stay calm and centred when dealing with difficult situations. You can try mindfulness techniques such as meditation, yoga, or deep breathing exercises.

Focus on solutions, not problems - When your child is being difficult, it can be easy to focus on the problem and become frustrated. Instead, focus on finding a solution to the problem. Ask yourself, "What can I do to help my child in this situation?" This can help you stay calm and focused on finding a positive outcome.

Seek support - Parenting can be a challenging and isolating experience, but it doesn't have to be. Reach out to friends, family, or a support group for help and guidance. Talking to someone who understands what you're going through can help you feel less alone and more supported.

In conclusion, keeping calm as a parent when dealing with young children is essential for maintaining a positive and healthy relationship with your child. By taking a deep breath, reminding yourself of your child's age and development, using positive self-talk, taking a break, practising mindfulness, focusing on solutions, and seeking support, you can stay calm and composed during difficult situations. Remember, parenting is a journey, and it takes time, effort, and patience to develop a strong and positive relationship with your child.

5 FOSTERING PSYCHOLOGICAL SAFETY AND EMOTIONAL WELL-BEING

Nasreen Bashraheel

The significance of the role adults play in children's lives, health, and well-being, we know, is huge. Parents and carers have a responsibility to ensure that children enjoy psychological safety and develop emotional well-being.

Without these two essential components, children can become vulnerable to feeling inadequate, and anxious and develop low self-esteem to the point where they feel that the world around them is such that they cannot freely express themselves. No one is interested in what they say and feel and when they do seek to make their point or make a contribution, it is ridiculed and criticised.

Psychological safety and emotional well-being are essential for developing a sense of self-worth and self-efficacy where the child learns what they can and can't do and builds the courage and confidence to develop their skills and knowledge and importantly, have the confidence to apply those skills.

This chapter is separated into two sections; psychological safety and emotional well-being.

Here we explore the role that you and your child's mental toughness and mental sensitivity play in creating a sense of psychological safety and emotional well-being.

As parents, we create many, if not most of the experiences that help to shape a child's mental toughness and through that, influence their sense of psychological safety and emotional well-being

This means that we can help our children learn to become confident, positive, optimistic and feel worthwhile in pursuit of becoming individuals with a sense of purpose who achieve what they can and build the resilience to deal with the stresses of life and seize the opportunities it can present.

A lack of psychological safety and emotional well-being in childhood can impact children's development throughout their lives. Not only is academic achievement impacted as is developing skills and attitudes, but so are future relationships and mental health.

What Is Psychological Safety?

Psychological safety exists when children feel they can safely express themselves, be themselves, and engage in interactions and experiences in their life without the fear of losing their sense of self, their sense of control and stability.

Having the freedom to express themselves means children can influence and direct their own thoughts and behaviours and learn how to deal with the consequences these have on their lives.

Why Is Psychological Safety Important?

Psychological safety is important because:

1. It creates the environment to prosper; and
2. It helps the child to develop to engage with others

Let's explore these further.

Creating an environment where a child can thrive and prosper is crucial for psychological safety. A child needs emotional support, sensory experiences, safe spaces, routines, and a parent who is present if they are to prosper both in the home and outside it.

Research has shown, that having what is considered to be self-regulation, and the mindset to positively take risks in life, and learn from all that happens when you do, is central to the way we develop as fully functioning human beings.

For children, feeling psychologically safe means that they can take risks in their lives without the fear of embarrassment, ridicule, or shame if they don't work out as expected. We understand that taking even moderate risks such as trying to do new things, meeting new people, picking up new experiences, etc. could lead to setbacks or failure.

Similarly, expressing a view or an opinion can mean that others may not agree or that the views are not sufficiently formed or evidenced to be accepted by others. Indeed, they can be rebuffed forcefully.

Children who have psychological safety grow up to become secure adults. Some other benefits of building psychological safety include:

- They do better academically
- They thrive as adults
- They build more stable and secure relationships
- They are not afraid to voice their opinions
- They develop self-identity
- They have better self-confidence and self-esteem

Children who experience psychological safety feel it is safe to try new things and take risks, and be able to accept the consequences as a normal part of their learning and development.

That means, using self-regulation to make decisions and take actions knowing that they feel psychologically safe.

Psychological safety enables children (who go on to become adults) to overcome barriers they face when it comes to learning and development. Psychological safety also refers to the perception people have of the consequences of taking interpersonal risks in life.

Research shows psychological safety is essential for children and adults to 'employ or express themselves physically, cognitively, emotionally...'. A lack of psychological safety can therefore lead to disengagement and lack of a 'sense of self'.

We can think of psychological safety as having two dimensions:

Firstly, creating an environment where a person can do things and express themselves without that fear of ridicule, rejection, etc. However, it is possible to create and support that environment and find that the individual still hesitates or is fearful to do the things that you would encourage them to do.

The second dimension is to understand and explore the mental responses of the child when pressed or encouraged to do or say things.

Parents are key drivers and conduits of psychological safety for children. Parents are instrumental in creating a child's first environment – the home. Within the home psychological safety enables the child to feel safe, build their sense of self, and flourish.

Parents play an important role in giving a child a sense of psychological safety by building their self-esteem and creating a safe environment within the home for the child to express themselves and learn (Edmondson, 2004).

The home, therefore, needs to become a therapeutic space that facilitates emotional growth and development.

Parents also have a role and responsibility to ensure that this exists wherever they expose their children. This includes nurseries, schools, clubs, playgroups, etc.

When we look at the individual perspective, that is, how each child responds, this is where the mental toughness concept matters the most. Refer to Chapter Two for a full description of the mental toughness model.

How To Recognise a Lack of Psychological Safety

Parents need to learn how to recognise a lack of psychological safety. The main way of doing this is to be present and engaged with the child. Look out for these signs in your child:

- Your child is withdrawing and not participating in activities
- Your child is overly emotional and irritable
- Your child exhibits fear and anxiety
- Your child is avoiding people and situations

If you notice any of these signs you must speak to the child and importantly listen to the responses.

Developing Psychological Safety

Here are some tips for creating psychological safety:

- Do not diminish or dismiss your child's fears and worries
- Validate their concerns through your words, non-verbal

communication (hugs and kisses), and actions
- Empathise with your child
- Build trust
- Offer your child love and reassurance
- Engage them by asking them open questions and building their confidence

Some things parents can say:

If your child is appearing withdrawn and anxious then there are some things you can do and say to help them:

- "Hey, are you ok today?"
- "It's ok to feel sad"
- "I understand and I am here for you"
- "I love you"
- "Shall we sit and cuddle for a while"
- "Do you want to play"
- "It's ok, we'll figure this out"

Emotional Well-being

What Is Emotional Well-being?

Emotional well-being is about understanding and managing emotions. Children who have emotional well-being can regulate their emotions well, cope with challenges and difficulties in their lives, and develop secure relationships.

Some children will learn to manage their emotions and even channel them for some benefit. Some don't do this and allow their emotions to dictate their response and their actions. They can reveal their emotional state to others – when it isn't always appropriate to do so.

Just like with the Emotional Control factor of the Mental

Toughness Model, this is not about not experiencing emotions. It is very much about effectively managing emotions.

Feeling psychologically safe enables children to build their resilience and their emotional well-being. Parents who create a loving and nurturing environment within which to raise their children essentially lay the foundation for improved mental health and well-being.

Why is Emotional Well-being Important?

Children need emotional well-being as it facilitates an understanding and awareness within them of their feelings, the potential consequences of those feelings and to become aware of strategies to manage those feelings.

Emotional well-being is also important for physical health (World Health Organisation). When there is a lack of emotional well-being, this impacts the physical health of the child.

In addition, children who lack emotional well-being may find that their development of personal, emotional, social and cognitive skills are impacted. This becomes apparent as they transition through life into adulthood and the different roles they play in their lives. Children who have formed secure attachments with caregivers can cope better with the challenges and stresses they face in life.

Fostering emotional well-being in childhood enables children to develop resilience and positivity to cope with difficult situations through school and adulthood. Families, particularly parents and caregivers, play a central role in developing emotional well-being in children.

Emotional well-being enables children to build secure and dependable relationships with their peers and adults in their lives. Furthermore, it means children can develop their own independence, life skills, social skills, express and manage their own feelings, and build their confidence and ability to deal with adversity.

Role of Parents and Carers – The Mental Toughness Dimension

Why can parents struggle here?

Parents may well have mastered a degree of emotional well-being and are psychologically secure but they can often forget that their children are not at that stage in their development. Parents can sometimes judge children by the standards expected of an adult.

"I don't know why they have done that; I wouldn't do it".

So, parents need to be aware of their own mental toughness and mental sensitivity to understand why they respond to their children the way they do. And from that learn how they can manage that better. This is covered in more detail in Chapter 2.

A child is on the journey towards adulthood and cannot be reasonably expected to have similar levels of mental toughness. We know, from studies in the UK that 10-year-old children, on average score 4.0 – 4.2 on the same scale. This is significantly different from an adult.

It is likely that 30% - 40% of children below the age of 10 have levels of mental toughness that would be described as mentally sensitive.

A mentally sensitive individual is likely to be sensitive to what others say and do and, is less likely to enjoy the levels of psychological safety that a more mentally tough individual might experience.

Indeed, studies also show that the average level for a 17-year-old in their last year in high school is around 4.5.

Mental Toughness and Emotional Well-being

Mental toughness enables children to develop good emotional well-being. Both of these concepts are closely linked. If we can teach our children mental toughness, this enables them to develop the skills they need to cope with adversity. In turn, this means they can manage their emotions better and promote self-resilience and well-being.

Mental toughness helps with developing emotional regulation and being able to understand our feelings better. This greater self-awareness leads to better emotional well-being.

As a parent, it is important to have self-awareness when it comes to your own mental toughness and your ability to channel that into providing psychological safety. Knowing the limits of our own mental toughness is essential because it helps us to develop our emotional responses, our control over our lives, and confidence in our ability as parents.

The mental toughness framework can be very useful to create this self-awareness in the parent and the child. Parents can, very usefully, also complete the MTQPlus assessment to measure their mental toughness. Refer to Chapter 14 for more details.

The image on the following page shows how the framework can signpost to understanding and development needs.

Mental Toughness and Psychological Safety

When you don't have it, each factor explains to what extent...

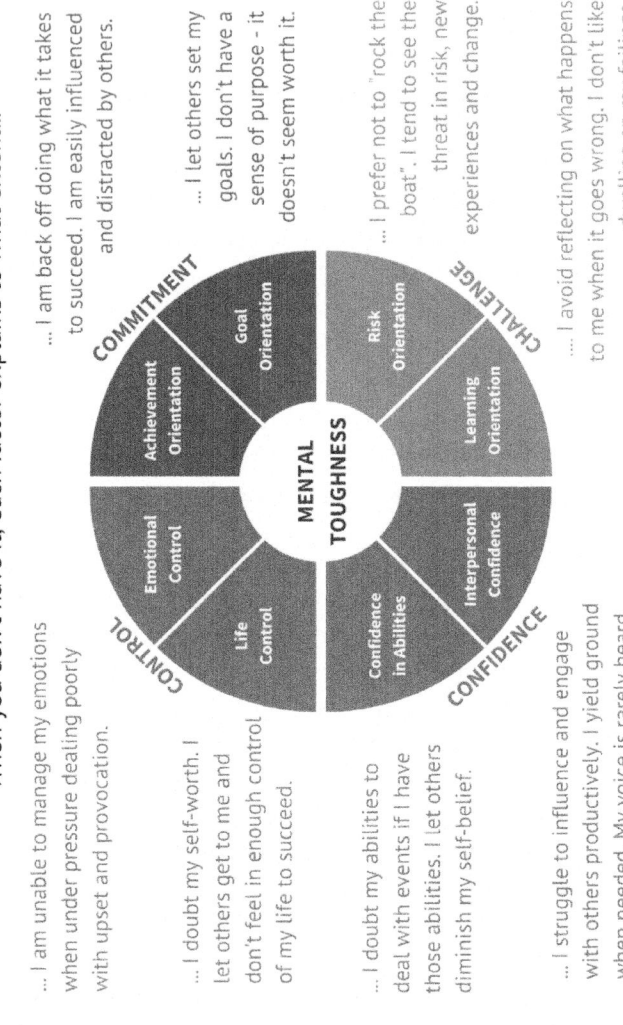

... I am unable to manage my emotions when under pressure dealing poorly with upset and provocation.

... I doubt my self-worth. I let others get to me and don't feel in enough control of my life to succeed.

... I doubt my abilities to deal with events if I have those abilities. I let others diminish my self-belief.

... I struggle to influence and engage with others productively. I yield ground when needed. My voice is rarely heard.

... I am back off doing what it takes to succeed. I am easily influenced and distracted by others.

... I let others set my goals. I don't have a sense of purpose - it doesn't seem worth it.

... I prefer not to "rock the boat". I tend to see the threat in risk, new experiences and change.

... I avoid reflecting on what happens to me when it goes wrong. I don't like dwelling on my failings.

***Fig. 4**: Psychological safety*

Parenting or/and caregiving is hard work, so it is important to know your own boundaries and limits, and where possible to work on strengthening yourself and being compassionate. This will help you avoid burnout and will enable you to provide psychological safety for yourself and your child.

The same framework can provide insight into understanding what a lack of psychological safety might mean for the development of a person. Careful reflection can help to identify what might be the areas for development for me, a parent, and/or my children.

Development suggestions are offered elsewhere in this book.

The Parent-child Relationship and Psychological Safety

The role parents and carers play in building a child's sense of psychological safety and emotional well-being is of paramount importance.

The root of a child's emotional well-being and sense of safety can be traced back to the parental attachments they have in their lives. Parental attachment refers to a very specific aspect of the parent-child relationship. Attachment between the parent and child helps children to feel secure, safe and protected by their parents. Attachment provides a child with a secure foundation or base from which to learn and explore. This base acts as a source of support and comfort for the child.

Parental relationships can often determine the child's sense of self, and this in turn can link to the child's internal stress management and regulation system.

Adequate and appropriate levels of attachment are critical for children if secure foundations and emotional well-being are to be created for a child.

As noted earlier, a parent's own emotional well-being and mental and physical health can impact the child's emotional well-being and psychological safety. The quality of the relationship between the parent and the child is at the core of the child's emotional well-being.

Parents and carers lay the foundations of the child's health and emotional well-being, and if there are issues in these early foundations these can impact the child as they become adults and try and build on these flawed foundations.

At the core of emotional well-being is the building of self-esteem and an awareness of emotions and how to manage them. This is best done in an environment where the child feels psychologically safe. Psychological safety provides the child with the psychological tools they need to build their emotional well-being and long-term resilience.

Within the home, children should be made to feel able to question, make mistakes, be creative and engage without fear of failure. This makes them feel psychologically safe.

Importance of Secure Relationships and Their Impact on Psychological Safety and Emotional Well-being

Secure parental relationships are developed when caregivers are emotionally and physically available to meet the needs of the child within their care. Developing a secure relationship not only creates a psychologically safe environment for the child but also helps them to strengthen their emotional well-being.

Developing emotional well-being helps children as they grow, whether that is in school environments, relationships with others, or professional environments. Children who benefit from secure relationships then go on to develop secure relationships of their own. This means they can take interpersonal risks and successfully transition and adapt to major life changes.

Parents who provide unconditional love consistently and lovingly enable children to engage with and develop their self-belief. This is important if children are to engage with the world and others around them. Parents and carers are instrumental in ensuring that the children in their care can build their self-esteem and self-worth. Using the Mental Toughness Framework is a key resource that helps develop self-esteem and mental resilience.

Creating an environment within the child's home from birth where the child can explore new experiences, opportunities and challenges helps the child to feel psychologically secure. This in turn enhances their emotional well-being. A safe and secure home enables children to feel protected not only within their environment but also within the parent-child relationship.

Emotional security for children can be developed by parents through:

Shared activities	Positive praise	Being responsive	Setting meaningful goals	Having structure and boundaries	Being consistent	Patience
Making bubbles. Baking a cake. Camping out in the living room. Singing songs.	Well done. Good job. It's fun playing with you. Wow, that's great.	Make eye contact. Smile. Encourage them listen to what they are saying. Ask questions.	Ask questions to learn about them. Read with them, aiming to finish the story. Make time for activities.	Have time set aside for play, learning, relaxing and bedtime. Have meals.	Have routines such as bath, pyjamas, bedtime story. Set ground rules. Be patient.	Listen to what they are saying and asking. Keep calm. Crouch down to their level.

Table 1 *Developing emotional security for children*

Of course, mental toughness, resilience and positivity are not only about giving the child opportunity and love. It also means that children learn to engage and build secure relationships in later life, living authentically as themselves, and building coping mechanisms for future challenges.

Protective Strategies of Children

Children who are more mentally sensitive may develop other protective strategies to deal with adversity. At this stage in their development, more young children have areas of mental sensitivity than they have of mental toughness. So, it is important to be very aware of this.

They may develop low self-esteem and confidence and become emotionally withdrawn, scared to do things or make mistakes, worried about failure, and stop engaging with those around them.

This is why, parents must learn about mental toughness and explore the topic with their children.

When it comes to building mental toughness, the four 'Cs' are important:

Control

Being in control of emotions during turbulent times enables mentally tough people to remain calm and controlled instead of distracted and destructive. It also means that they can control their ability to take risks and not talk themselves out of every possible 'risky' life situation (Clough et al, 2002).

Commitment

Commitment relates to goals and reliability. Someone with

commitment will set goals and commit to delivering them. Committing requires a degree of resilience, so those people who can commit tend to have good resilience and mental toughness. Commitment also enhances engagement in life and reduces the sense of alienation.

Challenge

Individuals who can challenge others and their own boundaries can assess and accept risk, and effect change in their lives. Having the confidence to challenge also involves the emotional foresight to assess outcomes and deal with the outcome. Mentally tough individuals do not shy away from challenges or become overwhelmed by them, instead, they see challenges as opportunities to grow, learn and experience.

Confidence

Confidence is about self-esteem and self-belief. As mentioned above, secure relationships and attachments lead to improved self-belief and emotional well-being. When confidence is developed in the context of psychological safety, it enables the child to build their internal confidence so that they can deal with challenges and conflicts in their lives.

There are various ways in which parents and carers can promote mental toughness to support their child's psychological well-being and emotional well-being including:

Here are some tips for creating psychological safety:

- Provide a safe home environment in which the child can question, learn, grow and develop.
- Learn to recognise attitudes and behaviour and how to help the child to reflect on these.
- Teach children how to understand and regulate their

emotions.
- Demonstrate positive behaviours yourself as a parent.
- Help children to manage and mitigate negative thoughts and behaviours.
- Teach your children it is okay to take risks and face fears (it's okay not to be okay).
- Let your children make mistakes and learn from them.
- Encourage healthy self-esteem and language around self.
- Storytelling can be a very powerful technique. Through the use of metaphors, the Resilient Hedgehog books used the mental toughness framework to build resilience and positivity in children.

Providing a safe space for children to develop mental toughness helps them to control their emotions healthily.

Children who do not develop mental toughness may remain mentally sensitive. Whilst mental sensitivity carries its advantages, it can also mean that a child feels every bump in the road. It may leave them open to uncertainty, anxiety, worries, and feelings of being out of control.

Not all children learn to develop mental toughness across the 4Cs. They are who they are but we can teach them how to cope with aspects of who they are and this can be equally effective.

Most people have a degree of mental toughness in some respects and a degree of mental sensitivity in others.

For many, it is about learning to grow and learning to manage what they cannot change.

If you do have a child who shows signs of mental sensitivity then there are some things you can do to help them.

First of all, you must actively listen to them to understand their sensitivity and what it means in practice – for example, do they worry about things that others don't? If it is something like 'I am worried about playing in the playground' then the parent should use positive, affirmative language such as, "It's ok to be worried, but there is nothing to be worried about because you will get to play with other children". It may also mean accepting that at times the child may happily play on their own or with a very small circle of friends.

Parents should focus on providing their children with the sense of safety they need to process and regulate their emotions. Providing context and a realistic approach will help the child feel more in control and commit to the thing they are scared of.

For example, talk about the positive outcomes of play, and the friends they could make, but also acknowledge that it is scary and see if you can help ease them into the situation as they build their resilience.

Supporting children in managing and regulating their behaviours and worries means that they will be able to deal with challenging situations and build their internal confidence and resilience.

Emotional well-being builds resilience, and this in turn builds emotional growth and stability. Where there is a lack of psychological safety for a child to build resilience, this can often lead to poor engagement with others, unrealistic expectations, pressure, and a fear of failure.

Conclusion

Parents who hold psychologically safe spaces for their children should aim to demonstrate their own emotional well-being and resilience in their behaviour. They should act as role models, modelling the behaviours they want the child to learn and develop.

Psychological safety and emotional well-being developed in childhood can reap benefits far beyond childhood, and from an individual to a societal level. When people can take interpersonal risks without feeling fearful and afraid, they are better able to deal with any ensuing failures and difficulties.

Children face immense pressures as they move through the world, from learning how to walk and talk, to starting school, dealing with peer pressures, societal expectations, exam pressures, and entering the professional realm.

Developing aspects of mental toughness not only prepares them to cope with these challenges but also equips them to build their own strategies for protecting their emotional well-being as they age.

Mental Toughness embraces resilience and positivity. Resilience enables us to manage adversity and setbacks. Positivity enables us to recognise opportunities ahead of us and the belief that we can grasp these. Both to a person's ability to manage effectively in situations of change and stress.

Of course, addressing mental toughness also enhances a person's ability to be successful as they become able to rationalise, re-energise, and rehabilitate themselves.

Enabling us to create psychological safety for ourselves and others that enables all "to become the best version of ourselves that we can be". Every parent's dream.

6 DEALING WITH CHILDREN'S BEHAVIOUR

Anna Golawski

Why do children misbehave?

This chapter is going to have a look at mental toughness and its link to children's behaviour. It will cover some of the reasons underlying the behaviours and coping strategies to support children for positive affect.

There are many reasons why children misbehave, and parents and caregivers need to understand these underlying reasons to effectively manage and prevent misbehaviour. Here are some common reasons why children misbehave:

Attention-seeking: Children may misbehave to get attention from adults, especially if they feel like they are not getting enough positive attention.

Boredom: Children may misbehave out of boredom, especially if they are not engaged in stimulating activities or given enough opportunities to play and explore.

Testing boundaries: Children may misbehave to test boundaries and see how far they can push limits. This is a normal part of development as children learn about the world around them and their place in it.

Frustration: Children may misbehave when they are frustrated, especially if they don't have the words or skills to express their emotions effectively.

Lack of structure: Children may misbehave if they don't have clear rules and expectations to follow, or if they don't have consistent routines and schedules.

Physical or emotional discomfort: Children may misbehave if they are experiencing physical discomforts, such as hunger or fatigue, or if they are struggling with emotional issues such as anxiety or stress.

Developmental issues: Children may misbehave if they have developmental issues such as ADHD or sensory processing disorder, which can make it difficult for them to regulate their behaviour and emotions.

It's important to keep in mind that misbehaviour is often a symptom of an underlying issue, rather than a deliberate attempt to be "bad" or "naughty". By understanding the reasons why children misbehave, parents and caregivers, can address these underlying issues and develop strategies to prevent and manage misbehaviour. This can involve creating a supportive and structured environment, providing opportunities for positive attention and engagement, setting clear and consistent rules and expectations, and helping children develop emotional regulation and problem-solving skills.

Mental toughness and behaviour

Mental toughness and misbehaviour in children may not be directly related, as mental toughness is generally associated with positive attributes such as resilience, perseverance, and self-confidence, while naughty behaviour is considered disruptive, disobedient, or problematic. However, mental toughness can help children regulate their emotions and behaviours better, which can reduce the likelihood of unwanted behaviour.

For example, a child with high levels of mental toughness may be better equipped to handle frustration or disappointment, which can reduce the likelihood of acting out in a disruptive or disobedient manner. Additionally, mental toughness can help children develop better coping skills and problem-solving abilities, which can enable them to address the underlying causes of their naughty behaviour and find more constructive ways to express themselves.

However, it's important to note that many factors can contribute to unwanted or misbehaviour in children, such as environmental factors, family dynamics, and individual temperament. While mental toughness can be a valuable asset for children in many ways, it may not necessarily be the sole or primary factor that influences naughty behaviour. It's important to address the underlying causes of behaviour and provide appropriate support and guidance to help children develop positive attitudes and behaviours.

The potential positive links to mental toughness are:

Control – being able to better control frustration, anger or anxiety so that emotions don't overwhelm them and lead to unwanted behaviours.

Commitment – having the tenacity to keep going with school projects or revision without giving up quickly or being easily distracted. However, if the level is too high, then the commitment to studies could be at the expense of other social or physical activities and interests.

Confidence - children who score high then have the confidence to make new friends and contribute positively to class discussions and activities.

Challenge – high scores tend to suggest they are likely to give new things a go and learn from new experiences.

Although there are many positives to children's behaviours, managing young children's unwanted or disruptive behaviour can be challenging, especially when they are angry, anxious, or aggressive. In addition, parents often face push-pull power struggles with their children, which can make it even more difficult to manage their behaviour effectively. In this chapter, we will discuss strategies for managing young children's behaviour, including how to address anger, anxiety, and aggression, and how to manage power struggles.

Addressing Anger, Anxiety, and Aggression

Young children often have difficulty managing their emotions, and may exhibit anger, anxiety, or aggression when they feel overwhelmed or stressed. Here are some strategies for addressing these behaviours:

Teach emotional regulation: Help your child learn how to identify and regulate their emotions. This can include teaching them deep breathing techniques, mindfulness exercises, or other relaxation techniques.

Provide structure and routine: Children feel more secure and less anxious when they have a predictable routine and structure in their daily lives. Create a consistent schedule for meals, bedtime, and other activities to help your child feel more secure.

Use positive reinforcement: Praise your child for positive behaviour and accomplishments, which can help boost their self-esteem and reduce anxiety.

Be a role model: Model appropriate behaviour and emotional regulation for your child, which can help them learn how to manage their own emotions.

Seek professional help: If your child's behaviour is severe or persistent, or if you are concerned about their emotional well-being, seek professional help from a therapist or counsellor.

Managing Power Struggles

Power struggles can arise between parents and young children, especially as children begin to assert their independence and test boundaries. Here are some strategies for managing power struggles:

Set clear expectations: Clearly communicate your expectations to your child, and be consistent in enforcing rules and consequences.

Offer choices: Provide your child with choices whenever possible, which can help them feel more in control and reduce the likelihood of power struggles.

Avoid power struggles: If your child refuses to comply with a rule or request, avoid engaging in a power struggle. Instead, offer a choice or redirect their attention to another activity.

Use natural consequences: When your child misbehaves, use natural consequences that are related to their behaviour, such as taking away a toy if they refuse to share.

Be empathetic: Try to understand your child's perspective and emotions and respond with empathy and understanding.

Use humour: Use humour and playfulness to diffuse tension and reduce the likelihood of power struggles.

It can be challenging to tell the difference between young children who are misbehaving because they are attention seeking versus attention needing. Here are some signs to look for:

Attention-Seeking Behaviours:

Inappropriate behaviour: Children who are seeking attention may engage in inappropriate behaviour, such as acting out or breaking rules.

Negative attention seeking: Children may seek attention through negative behaviours, such as throwing a tantrum or being rude to others.

Lack of concern for others: Children who are seeking attention may not be concerned with the impact of their behaviour on others and may continue to engage in negative behaviours even when others are upset or hurt.

Short-lived behaviours: Attention-seeking behaviours may be short-lived and may stop once the child receives attention.

Attention-Needing Behaviours:

Need for validation: Children who are attention-needing may need validation and affirmation from others and may engage in behaviours that elicit positive attention.

Repeated behaviours: Children who are attention needing may engage in the same behaviours repeatedly, as they are seeking ongoing validation and attention.

Need for connection: Children who are attention-needing may have a deep need for connection with others and may engage in behaviours that help them feel more connected and valued.

Positive behaviours: Attention-needing behaviours may include positive behaviours, such as seeking out activities or interactions that bring them positive attention.

If you are unsure whether your child's behaviour is attention seeking or attention needing, it can be helpful to observe their behaviour over time and to seek the advice of a mental health professional or paediatrician. They can provide insight and guidance on how to best support your child's emotional and social needs. Remember that all children have unique personalities and needs, and it is important to approach each child with empathy and understanding.

Dealing with refusing to go to school

As a parent, it can be difficult to manage your child's behaviour when they refuse to go to school. It can be frustrating and overwhelming to deal with this situation, but it is important to approach it calmly and constructively. Here are some tips on how to manage your child's behaviour when they are refusing to go to school.

Understand the underlying reasons: There may be underlying reasons why your child is refusing to go to school. It could be due to anxiety, bullying, academic struggles, or a lack of motivation. It is essential to understand the root cause of their behaviour before trying to address it.

Communicate with your child: Talk to your child and ask them why they don't want to go to school. Listen to their concerns and try to understand their perspective. You can also explain to them the importance of attending school and how it can benefit them in the long run.

Set clear expectations: Set clear expectations with your child that attending school is non-negotiable. Let them know that you expect them to attend school regularly and on time. You can also set consequences for not attending school, such as losing privileges or facing disciplinary action.

Establish a routine: Establish a routine for your child to follow every day. This can include waking up at the same time, eating breakfast, and getting dressed. Having a routine can help your child feel more organised and prepared for the day ahead.

Offer support Offer: support and encouragement to your child as they transition back to school. Let them know that you are there for them and that you believe in their ability to succeed. You can also offer to help them with their schoolwork or connect them with resources such as tutors or counselling services.

Work with the school: Work with your child's school to address any issues or concerns that may be contributing to their refusal to attend school. This can include meeting with teachers, counsellors, or administrators to develop a plan to support your child's academic and social-emotional needs.

Celebrate progress: Celebrate your child's progress and achievements, no matter how small. Recognise their efforts and praise them for their hard work. This can help build their confidence and motivation to continue attending school.

Managing your child's behaviour when they refuse to go to school requires patience, understanding, and clear communication. By understanding the underlying reasons, communicating with your child, setting clear expectations, establishing a routine, offering support, working with the school, and celebrating progress, you can help your child overcome their reluctance to attend school and achieve academic success. Remember, every child is different, and it may take time to find the right approach that works for your child. Be patient and persistent, and your child will eventually thrive in their academic and social environment.

Conclusion

Managing young children's behaviour can be challenging, but it is an important part of parenting. By understanding the underlying reasons for behaviour, such as anger, anxiety, and aggression, and using effective strategies for managing power struggles, parents can create a positive and supportive environment for their children to thrive. Remember to be patient, consistent, and empathetic, and seek professional help if needed. With time and effort, parents can help their children develop the emotional regulation and social skills needed to succeed in life.

7 SUPPORTING THE DEVELOPMENT OF POSITIVE PEER RELATIONSHIPS

Toni Molyneux

This chapter is going to explore peer relationships and how they relate to the eight factors that make up a person's mental toughness. It will also briefly explore some suggestions for developing mental toughness in relation to peer relationships.

During the earlier years of a child's life, their parents shape and influence their experiences. Once a child starts at nursery or school, teachers and peers begin to have more of an influence on experiences, with the latter becoming more influential as they age. Naturally, any parent or guardian worries about whether their child will 'fit in' at school and make friends. As a child enters adolescence, the focus of those worries shifts towards the negative impacts associated with peer pressure. These worries are normal.

As a parent, you will want to do all you can to support your child in establishing positive peer relationships. It can be difficult to find the balance between wanting to protect your child and allowing them the autonomy to explore, try new things and learn. There is a temptation to want to wrap your child up in cotton wool and protect them from things that might potentially cause them harm or upset. However, we can't protect them from everything. This kind of approach can lead to a risk-averse culture, and it can take away any opportunities a child has to learn, grow and develop a sense of mental toughness – to help them deal with life challenges and obstacles.

The Mental toughness framework can help to support you as a parent or guardian and support your children to deal with the challenges and opportunities faced in life and in particular, as we will discuss here, in establishing and maintaining positive peer relationships.

Let's start by examining what we mean by peer relationships. "Peer relationships are interpersonal relationships established and developed during social interactions among peers or individuals with similar levels of psychological development (La Greca & Harrison, 2005). Peer relationships are very different from relationships with adults. The relationship between a child and an adult is vertical - the adult is in charge and that is largely accepted. Relationships with peers tend to be more balanced without a clear line of dominance.

Children form many types of peer relationships including friendships with children of a similar age or developmental level, mentoring relationships where they can look to older children to learn, peer groups with which they share common interests and activities (like sports teams and hobbies), cliques (exclusive groups with a close bond) and rival groups where children may compete or have some form of conflict. Each type of relationship will impact a child's development in different ways which is often dependent on the time spent and the quality of the relationships formed.

Why are peer relationships important?

Influences from peer relationships begin in the first years of life and by three years of age, children show preferences for specific peers (Hay, Payne & Chadwick, 2004). Peer relationships play a key role in shaping the social, emotional, moral and ethical development of children; impacting school experience and performance, behaviour and health. Some of the effects (both positive and negative) of peer relationships in childhood may be temporary, while others may be permanent and affect a person throughout their life.

Peer relationships provide a great deal of learning and

development opportunities such as learning to share, getting along with others and how to take turns, learning to be altruistic and developing empathy. They also provide a safe and secure place for children to explore, learn how to problem solve, resolve conflicts and understand social cues. Peer relationships allow children to learn how to communicate effectively and provide a place for them to express their feelings. They help to shape a child's moral and ethical development.

Friendships of high quality, provide a sense of well-being, caring, companionship and support, as well as often sought-after peer validation, boosting self-confidence. Peer relationships come in many forms and can have a positive or negative impact.

The increasing availability of technology at a younger age and as children develop has given nuance to how children form peer relationships, how they are maintained and the quality of those relationships. Technology has many advantages, allowing people to connect with others when they are not physically able to do so and providing the opportunity to connect with more people.

Despite bringing some advantages, technology changes how peer relationships are formed and maintained. They are more difficult to develop, tend to have less depth and are of a lower quality than face-to-face friendships (Baiocco, Cacioppo, Laghi & Tafià., 2011). Technology can also be detrimental, exposing children to the risk of cyberbullying and feelings of isolation and exclusion. It is therefore vitally important to prepare children to deal with these challenges.

As is the case with all forms of development, some children may develop peer relationships quicker and they may establish stronger relationships, whereas others may experience difficulties. For some, those difficulties may be minor and pose no major implications. For others, those difficulties may be greater and pose more substantial challenges. Difficulties forming peer relationships can result in delinquency, dropping out of school, emotional problems and adjustment issues later in life. Therefore, it is important to support your child in forming positive childhood peer relationships and equipping them with the skills needed to deal with stressful events. If you are unsure or concerned it is advisable to seek help from a healthcare professional.

As ever, be mindful not to compare your child to others. As previously mentioned throughout this book, self-awareness is important. It is about understanding strengths and limitations and what implications this has on a person's circumstances. It is about helping your child to be the best version of themselves.

Mental Toughness and Peer Relationships

When we examine the role that Mental Toughness plays in peer relationships, it must be kept in mind that children tend to be more mentally sensitive.

The Mental Toughness of a child can have a great impact on their peer relationships. Children with high levels of mental toughness are more self-aware; they tend to be better at handling difficult people and situations and do so more confidently and positively. This can help when developing positive high-quality relationships with peers.

For example, children with a stronger sense of mental toughness may be better at resolving conflict, making positive choices and communicating openly. Because they have a belief that they can influence much of the world in which they operate, they tend to be less vulnerable to negative peer pressure and may be better at setting boundaries. They may be more comfortable with who they are, their interests and standing their ground.

The Mentally Tough (both adults and children) are more likely to recognise and ask for help and support from their peers when they may be struggling. That being said, this does not mean that those children who are more mentally sensitive will struggle entirely with forming or maintaining peer relationships; they may just require more support and guidance in preparing them for the challenges that come with forming and maintaining peer relationships and dealing with negative peer pressure.

We'll now take a deep dive into the factors that comprise mental toughness, examining how a person's sense of mental toughness in each regard may present and how it relates to peer relationships. Importantly, this section will also briefly touch upon things you can do as a parent to support your child. Further details can be found in chapters 13 and 14. You can refer to Chapter 2 for detailed descriptions of each factor.

Confidence

The simplest place to start is with Confidence. Confidence describes to what extent you believe you can deal with the challenges and opportunities you face.

Confidence in Abilities	I have self-belief in my abilities to deal with things.
Interpersonal Confidence	I am happy to engage with and to influence others.

Confidence in Abilities

Confidence in Abilities describes the extent to which a person has self-belief in their abilities, knowledge and skills. Without this, a person may possess abilities but not have the confidence to use them.

For instance, despite that a child might demonstrate a clear capability in a subject area, they may not recognise this knowledge and will describe themselves as being "rubbish at it".

This lack of confidence in their ability can sometimes lead to a reluctance to answer questions (both verbally and written), they may hesitate more and question themselves. They may be more reluctant to ask questions or participate in discussions with their peers because it may make them feel "stupid". They may look more to their peers for advice, approval and validation of their knowledge.

Confidence in Abilities is also about whether a person feels worthwhile – their self-esteem, and if they require external validation of their abilities and skills. Sometimes children need a little reassurance and encouragement that they can do or achieve something, particularly if it is something they have never experienced before. In this case, those who are more mentally sensitive may require more external validation from their peers. They may look for the approval of their peers as confirmation of their skills and abilities. Those who are more mentally tough in this regard will be more confident about their skills and will rely less on their peers for validation. They know they are good and they are happy to show that to others.

For those children who have a strong sense of confidence in their abilities, this may come in the form of possessing an inner sense of self-belief and self-assurance. This may be beneficial in forming peer relationships and a child may be less likely to succumb to peer pressure. They will often have a go at most things meaning they may find forming new friendships easy. However, at times they may believe they are right even when they are wrong which could cause some conflict issues with peers.

Interpersonal Confidence

Interpersonal Confidence reflects the ability to deal confidently with people, particularly with challenging people. It's about being confident that you can influence and persuade others. A strong sense of Interpersonal Confidence can have a positive effect on peer relationships.

Those who have strong Interpersonal Confidence tend to be more assertive and take initiative which can aid them in forming strong peer relationships. For example, when visiting the local park, a child with a stronger sense of interpersonal confidence is more likely to be comfortable approaching other children, introducing themselves and playing with others.

They will be more likely to participate in discussions and ask questions, happily chatting with others, even those they don't know very well. Although, at times they may be at risk of overpowering others. They are more likely to stand their ground and face down any criticism which will be beneficial when faced with negative peer pressure.

Those with low Interpersonal Confidence may struggle to engage with their peers or to form new friendships. They won't always communicate their problems or worries, and they are at risk of not asking for clarification when they are unsure. They may wait for others to approach and engage with them first.

Children with low Interpersonal Confidence may be more vulnerable to peer pressure since they may be less likely to stand their ground. They may be more easily persuaded to do something they don't want to do because they are reluctant to speak up or go against the majority. When thinking about peer pressure, as parents, you may naturally think first about (and worry about) negative forms of peer pressure, however, this can come in both positive and negative forms. Being persuaded to try and experience new things – new experiences, food, culture, fashion etc can be beneficial for a child's development and finding who they are as a person.

There needs to be a balance established here between having

an appropriate level of Interpersonal Confidence to try new things and being comfortable enough in themselves and who they are to stand their ground and stick to their morals.

Control

Control describes to what extent you believe you control and shape what happens to you.

Life Control	I think I am worthwhile - I will "give most things a go".
Emotional Control	I can manage my emotions and make good decisions.

Life Control

Life Control describes the extent to which a person possesses a sense of self-worth. This enables them to manage many of the elements which affect their lives. It is about the extent to which a person feels in control of the factors that influence what they do and the extent to which they accept what they cannot control. This can be about managing the things that affect their performance at school or managing the things that don't make them feel great.

Much of a child's life is controlled by their parents and teachers – one aspect of fostering a sense of life control comes from encouraging a child to accept what they cannot control such as schoolwork, homework, school uniform etc. and managing how they respond to these situations. They can control their attitude and approach.

For a child, interactions with peers will play a significant role in their sense of life control.

Developing a strong sense of life control can help to provide a sense of security and acceptance. See Chapter 5 for more information on psychological safety and emotional well-being.

Those with a strong sense of Life Control will mostly cope well. They may approach most things in life with the belief that they can make things happen and make a difference. However, at times they may become frustrated if they feel that things don't go their way which may lead to potential peer conflicts - a challenge most parents face regularly as their child grapples to find their sense of life control and push their boundaries.

Those with a low sense of life control may often feel at the mercy of things and the people around them. They may believe that things just happen to them and may blame others, particularly their peers or outside factors.

Emotional Control

Emotional Control describes the extent to which a person can manage their emotional responses to events and those around them. Remember this does not mean that a person does not or should not experience certain emotions – it is about how they respond and manage those emotions when they arise. We all feel anxious, worried or frustrated at times, especially young children still learning to recognise what different emotions are, how they feel and what they mean.

Children who have strong emotional control may appear difficult to provoke or annoy and may appear impassive when others make comments that could upset or annoy them.

For example, if participating in a competitive sports game, a child may be exposed to comments from the opposing team which might seek to provoke them. In this case, those with good emotional management can effectively mask their emotions and appear unprovoked or unflappable to those around them. This does not mean that they do not feel frustrated or upset because of those actions, but they can effectively manage them and not let those emotions take over.

Those who are more mentally sensitive in this regard would readily reveal their emotions in the same situation. They would likely display emotional outbursts. For those who are mentally sensitive, it can be very difficult to manage their emotions according to the situation. This can result in conflicts with peers, placing strain on relationships and contributing to the formation of rival groups.

It's important to take a moment here to remember that children are more likely to be mentally sensitive than mentally tough. Many factors will affect their ability to manage their emotions such as hormonal changes, growth leaps etc., but for many, they will simply struggle to recognise and identify emotions. As a parent, you can support your child in this regard by helping them to identify and understand different emotions and what situations trigger them.

Commitment

Commitment refers to what extent a person will make promises and keep those promises.

Goal Orientation	I have self-belief in my abilities to deal with things.
Achievement Orientation	I am prepared to work hard & do what it takes to succeed.

Goal Orientation

Goal Orientation describes the extent to which an individual visualises goals and targets for their activities and outcomes. Goals provide purpose for many. What some children may see as goals and how they visualise them; how they look in their mind and what the outcome looks like, may be influenced by their peers and what their peers' goals are. This may be a driver behind their behaviour and attitude.

For example, what asked, "What do you want to be when you grow up?" There are of course a whole host of variables that influence this decision for a child. This will largely depend on what has been modelled around them – their parents, grandparents, aunts and uncles' careers, and what they have seen on TV or YouTube. However, those children with a high sense of goal orientation are more inclined to have a clearer view of what they want to be. To them, what their peers want to do for a career won't be so important. They are less likely to be distracted from their own goal. For those children who have a lower sense of goal orientation, their choice may be more influenced by their peers or look to them for influence.

Stepping away from peer relationships for a moment, this is a great opportunity to explore how a child's sense of goal orientation can have a great impact on their response to tests and exams. Those who are more mentally tough and enjoy setting and visualising goals may see tests and exams as an opportunity to show what they know, especially when coupled with a strong level of confidence in their abilities. They tend to be more focused, better able to maintain that focus and strive for more. They generally find exams and tests less stressful. Inversely, those who are more mentally sensitive will find exams and tests intimidating and may be overwhelmed.

A person's sense of goal orientation can have major implications on teamwork and goal alignment or in situations where they simply have no control over the goal, target or task.

Those who have a high goal orientation where they have a clear preference and view of their own goals and what that might look like may struggle when working towards a common goal with others.

For example, a group of children have been set a task – a

common goal that they must achieve, and they must work together to figure out and successfully achieve that task. Those who are less goal-orientated may find that situation easier. They may not have a strong view of what that goal looks like or how to achieve it, and they can rely on the support of their peers to figure that out. They are much happier to 'go with the flow' and are less likely to have a pressing view on what that should look like. This can help to foster positive relationships with peers. However, since they may be more likely to take a back seat rather than lead, they do have to be careful to not be seen as not contributing to the team or to appear passive which could result in peer conflict.

For those who are highly goal-orientated, this can be a stressful situation. They are likely to have their own view on what the task comprises, what that looks like and how to go about achieving it and that might not align with the rest of the group. This may place strain on relationships with their peers. However, it might also result in them taking the lead of the team. Their response will likely depend on the combination of their levels of mental toughness across other factors, for example, on their confidence in abilities and interpersonal confidence.

Some people may simply not think in terms of goals. However, possessing a degree of mental toughness in this regard carries advantages in many settings.

Achievement Orientation

Achievement Orientation describes the extent to which a person will do what it takes to achieve their own goals or to do what is asked of them. Remember that not everyone who visualises goals (goal orientation) necessarily puts in the work to achieve them. Think about people who set New Year's Resolutions – they may enjoy the process of setting and visualising goals for the year, but many don't see those goals through. Conversely, some who don't set goals may work hard when they have been asked to do something. This gives them a sense of purpose.

Children who have a high achievement orientation are generally able to maintain focus. When asked to do something, they are prepared to do what it takes to achieve that and to keep their commitment to others. This doesn't necessarily need to be a task in itself; it may be something as simple as a promise. This helps to foster positive peer relationships. Overall, they tend to be more tenacious and conscientious, being more aware of the impact of their actions on others. They will complete tasks even under difficult circumstances. Their peers will be aware that they can be relied upon. This is beneficial for fostering and maintaining healthy peer relationships.

Those who have a low achievement orientation find working toward goals and targets stressful. They may easily become bored and so won't commit time and effort. This can harm peer relationships. At times, this may frustrate their peers as it can appear as though they are disinterested, or they cannot be relied upon.

For example, those who have a lower achievement orientation may view promises more casually. Say, they may commit to a friend play together during their lunch break, however, when that time comes, something new may arise and they may become easily distracted by this and move on to something else. This may leave their friend feeling upset, although they mean no harm, they simply view promises casually – it doesn't matter if I keep that promise or not.

At times, those with low achievement orientation may convince themselves that something is not achievable and therefore they can be unwilling to sustain effort if they believe they cannot overcome a challenge. It is times like these that they may rely more on their peers for support.

Ultimately, this is something that will increase in importance as they grow older – for their exams, studies and then for their workplace relationships and success.

Challenge

The challenge component of Mental Toughness is about how a person sees and responds to challenges.

Risk Orientation	I see opportunity when exposed to new situations.
Learning Orientation	I think about all that happens to me and learn from that.

Risk Orientation

Risk Orientation describes the extent to which a person will mentally challenge themselves. It is about the extent to which they will take risks and explore outside of their comfort zone. As previously mentioned, risk orientation determines how a person responds to change or unplanned events. For some people, it is simply about the excitement that comes with experiencing new things.

A major source of change is the transition from preschool to school. Those who are more risk-oriented are likely to take this in their stride, even if it's something they find a little frightening. They are more likely to see it as an exciting chance to do something new. To them, the change may be thrilling. They therefore may settle in and form relationships with peers quicker.

Those who are more risk-averse may prefer a more safe and secure option. They'll want to stay within their comfort zone and stick with what they know. They generally dislike new situations. They may struggle more with the transition to school and therefore find it harder to develop relationships with their peers.

A high-risk orientation may come in the form of being easily bored and seeking or provoking change. They like being challenged and therefore tend to be more competitive. Those who are more risk-oriented may be more likely to engage in risky behaviours with their peers and may be more easily influenced. This may mean that generally, they are more able to form strong relationships and social connections with their peers.

Those who have a lower sense of risk orientation prefer a safe and secure world and may not like nor will they respond well to sudden changes. They may be less likely to be influenced into risky behaviours which may impact their ability to form strong relationships. However, they may have a better sense of who they are and what they like, not feeling a need to try new things. Having a low sense of risk orientation can bring both positives and negatives. They may be less pressured into risky behaviour, but they may not be exposed to or open to new experiences – to learn from their peers.

Of course, we are all exposed to risks, to change and to unplanned events in our lives, no matter our preference. As children, one of the biggest changes they will experience is the transition from primary to secondary education, pushing them out of their comfort zone. It is therefore imperative that children are provided with the tools they need to prepare for and manage those situations when they arise to ensure they are best equipped to be successful. For others, this may mean encouraging self-awareness. During these times, children who form stronger relationships are likely to rely more on their peers for support.

Learning Orientation

Learning Orientation describes the extent to which a person reflects on and learns from all experiences, whether that experience had a good or bad income.

For example, your child has joined a gymnastics club and they are excited to start classes and are confident that they can do well. However, their first class was more difficult than they had anticipated, and things didn't go too well. Maybe they struggled and they found it trickier than it looks! Maybe their excitement got the better of them and they struggled to focus and listen, and they walked away from their first class feeling a little disheartened.

Those high in learning orientation will see that as an opportunity to learn. They will reflect on the experience, thinking about how they can do better next time. They will try again, putting to use their newfound knowledge. They might practice at home. They are likely to look to their friends who can do these and learn from them. Whereas those with low learning orientation will easily give up without reflecting on the experience. Setbacks and failures can often shut them off meaning they won't try again. Their experience may put them off going back to gymnastics class altogether. This means that they may risk repeatedly making the same mistakes.

A high sense of learning orientation may come in the form of an improvement ethos. They see the positive in all outcomes, good or bad (for their own and their peers' experiences). They are keen to apply what they learn, enjoying trying things again or new situations. They like to test their knowledge.

Those with low learning orientation don't always see the bigger picture. They tend to have lower aspirations not recognising their own skillset. They may rely on validation from peers. When things go wrong, they may tend to blame others resulting in issues with peer relationships. As a parent, when you see your child struggling or making a mistake it is tempting to step in and help them. It is important to allow them to make small mistakes. Although it is tempting, don't come to their rescue immediately. Help them to focus on the solution instead and to reflect and learn from the experience. Encourage them to learn from their peers' experiences too and to look to them for support.

What can you do to support your child?

- Consciously seek to build up your child's feelings of self-worth through giving praise, appreciation and recognition when they achieve things. Encourage them to praise themselves; to recognise their achievements, even small ones. Activities like Think Three Positives and Making Affirmations are great for this (chapter 14).
- Teach your child to value themselves and to build their self-esteem. Encourage them to stand their ground, to voice their opinions and ideas and help them to discover themselves and their talents. Explore and practice assertiveness.
- Consider temporarily changing their environment to give new challenges that are not tainted by recent failures. Help to set them up for success but be careful not to wrap them in cotton wool. We become mentally tough through experience.
- Use storytelling to demonstrate mental toughness in action (see chapter 15).
- Support your child in finding what motivates and interests them and build this into the planning of tasks. To build the skills they need, start with the things they enjoy. They are less likely to give up for to become distracted.
- Encourage them to ask for help and guidance – from their parents and teachers as well as their peers.
- Have self-awareness – as a parent, you should be aware of your own mental toughness and model appropriate behaviour.

Conclusion

Any parent wants the best for their children and supporting them in developing positive peer relationships is crucial not just for their childhood experiences but in setting them up for a bright and prosperous future. It is tempting to want to wrap your child up in cotton wool and protect them from risks in life, to protect them from the negative aspects that can arise from peer relationships – things like bullying, delinquency etc. But this also stifles their ability to learn and grow – to experience new things, to learn through their peers, to explore new tastes in fashion and music and to develop their own sense of self. Striking that balance between fostering independence and protecting them is a natural worry.

Developing their mental toughness and building their self-awareness, their sense of self allows them to feel comfortable in forming and maintaining relationships with peers, trying new experiences and making and learning from mistakes. Importantly, it equips them to feel comfortable knowing and setting their boundaries and limits and to say no when they do not feel comfortable or feel they are being pressured into something that they do not like. These skills are crucial as a child's dependency on their parents decreases. It allows them to become self-sufficient.

8 UNDERSTANDING AND SUPPORTING THROUGH TRAUMA, ADVERSITY AND LOSS

Dorien van 't Ende and Maria Lawless

In this chapter, we are going to explore trauma, adversity, loss and bereavement. These are all challenges that children and adults will experience to varying degrees over a lifetime. Everyone is individual and his or her response to grief, loss, trauma and adversity will be unique. Children will need a responsive supportive adult to help them to deal with these situations. Connection is important for everyone going through challenges. Age-appropriate honesty is encouraged when dealing with these topics. Mental toughness can support us in supporting our children through the challenges life throws at us.

Loss is an inevitable part of life and comes in many forms. We will all have to deal with some kind of loss eventually in life. This can be a small loss, like losing a cherished possession, a bigger one, like a divorce or a friend moving away, or the biggest loss of all – the death of a pet or loved one. When someone dies, we often feel a range of emotions, like sadness, anger, despair, helplessness, numbness, etc.

The fact of the matter is that we will all have to deal with death at some point in our lives. Yet, when losing a loved one actually happens, many of us feel like we have no idea how to cope with it. Often, we are left wondering 'Why did nobody ever prepare me for this?'

There is no single right or wrong answer to this. It is, however, safe to say that many parents avoid the topic with their children simply because it can be upsetting for a child, the same way it is upsetting for most adults. No parent wants to hurt or worry their children. So, what is the easiest thing to do? Avoid the topic altogether - even if we know that might not be the best thing to do in the end. What do we do if a child loses a loved one and we can no longer avoid the topic? Dealing with loss is a difficult topic we often avoid talking about to not upset children. This can mean we may not learn to cope with it later in life.

Grief is as unique as our fingerprints. It is important to make a child familiar with these topics as it can help them later in life. If, as adults, we can support them with losing something that to us seems small, like a favourite toy, it may help them deal with bigger losses later in life. How we deal with loss will depend on many factors. Our connection with others and the support received is a factor. Throughout our lives and children's lives, change is a constant.

Allowing children to see our own sadness can be beneficial to their process. Often adults hide their upset in front of children to try and avoid upsetting the child. Children may be upset anyway but feel that they cannot talk about it if an adult is not talking about it. Children sometimes may fear that they will further upset the adult. A vicious cycle of unexpressed emotions can begin and continue for the child and adult. Both are trying to protect the other. Children will create their own stories if they are uninformed. They will sense that something is off and often the stories that they create can be even worse than the reality of the situation. Crying releases cortisol, the stress hormone from our bodies and it is a perfectly normal response to loss, sadness and adversity.

Acknowledging your own varied emotions and sharing this with a child can be helpful for the child. This shows that you are a safe space for them, can handle your own emotions and act as a safe container for your child's expression of emotions. Emotions are often labelled as 'good' and 'bad'. This can lead to children wanting to avoid sadness or anger, as these are labelled bad. Emotions are energy in motion and will come and go. Behaviour is a form of communication and children may express various behaviours in response to loss, adversity and trauma.

The acknowledgement and language around loss play a pivotal role. Age-appropriate use of language is an important factor in how children deal with loss and bereavement. Using honest and clear language in a child-appropriate way is important. Regarding children and bereavement, the best practice is to use clear, concise and simple language. Sometimes adults feel that they are protecting children by not using the words 'death' or 'died'. It is recommended to say '___ has died'. Younger children can take language quite literally and using terms like 'passed away' and 'gone to heaven' can confuse them.

This can make a child think their loved one may come back or make it seem that a loved one not being there is only a temporary situation. Some children may have no external reaction to a death but may be struggling to process it internally. You can see how they may get worried about going to sleep in the evening. Answer any questions truthfully. It is perfectly fine to say you do not have answers to certain questions.

Like adults, children will experience strong emotions when losing someone they care about. How children will respond to death depends on their age and their understanding of the concept. Babies and small children will not be able to understand death, but they may respond to the absence of an important person. They may be upset or extra clingy for a while and experience separation anxiety in certain situations.

Children between the ages of two and four will probably still struggle to understand the concept of death, and, in particular, that it is forever. They may say they know someone is dead, but at the same time ask when they will be seeing this person again. Death may also become a part of their play. School-age children may have a limited understanding of death as they are probably more likely to be exposed to it through watching TV and contact with other children. Some children may look for reasons to blame themselves for someone's death, so it is important to reassure them it is not their fault. They may be worried about monsters, fear the dark, worry their loved one is cold, in pain or alone, etc.

As a parent, you can respond by listening, answering questions, comforting, reassuring, being honest, revisiting the subject, and checking if a child understands. Use clear, concise language. Reflect back to the child what they said to be clear that you heard and understood what they were conveying. Allow children a safe way to express themselves. They can play, draw, and use puppets. They may not have the language to express their feelings but play is a safe way and developmentally appropriate. Use their interests and play to connect with them. "Toys are children's words and play is their language." Garry Landreth. "Birds fly, fish swim and children play." (Landreth, G 'Play Therapy: The Art of the Relationship 1991).

Trauma can be defined as an event that falls outside the range of usual human experience that causes distress. Trauma can be either human-made or from natural causes. Examples of human-made trauma include violence, war, car accidents, or witnessing the injury of someone else. Natural traumatic events might include floods, earthquakes, and volcanic eruptions.

How people experience trauma can be grouped into two types. These are commonly known as big T and little T. A big T event is one that most people would find traumatic such as a plane crash or a sudden unexpected loss of a loved one. A little T is a loss, that feels traumatic on a personal level such as the loss of a pet, or a relationship breakup. Our bodies respond to trauma by going through a variety of fight-or-flight responses. Our physiology is made up to protect us. When we are in this survival mode, our body is flooded with cortisol, which is the stress hormone.

When we experience trauma, our brain kicks into survival mode, which is known as 'fight or flight mode'. When we are in survival mode our brain cannot work to full capacity. The limbic system, which is the logical and reasoning part of our brain, shuts down. In an actual emergency, this is helpful. If we are being chased by a tiger we do not need to think about our feelings, we need adrenaline to get us to safety. Oftentimes, when people experience significant loss, adversity or trauma they are living in a state of survival and fight or flight.

Grief feels heavy in the body; it affects the lungs and energy reserves. Supporting someone through bereavement, trauma and loss is beneficial to the person. Everyday tasks can be challenging such as cooking, cleaning and having the capacity to look after ourselves properly.

"Being able to feel safe with other people is probably the single most important aspect of mental health; safe connections are fundamental to meaningful and satisfying lives." (Van der Kolk, B., 1994 'The Body Keeps the Score; Brain, Mind and Body in the Healing of Trauma).

We all experience challenges, setbacks and adversities in life. Through overcoming adversities, we have gained resilience. There are ten Adverse Childhood Experiences (ACEs), which can have an impact on children. These are physical abuse, sexual abuse, emotional abuse, physical neglect, emotional neglect, mental illness, divorce, substance abuse, violence against your mother and if a family member is in prison. Having experienced ACEs of four or more can have health implications in later life as these children become adults.

One good caring adult in a child's life can have a huge positive impact on their life. Dr Bruce Perry talks about post-traumatic wisdom in his book with Oprah 'What happened to you?'. He describes it as "the experience where you've been able to get through adversity and you're now at a safe place in your life and can look back and reflect," he says. "And take what you've learned and use that to see the world differently. You use your pain, transform it into power, and help other people. I think of the most transformative people I've ever known, every single one of them had personal pain and traumatic experience that was a core element of who they became." He goes on: "It didn't crush them…Those people tend to have tremendous empathy for those who are struggling. And they tend to have wisdom. They are wise about the ability to live with pain and not have so much fear from pain." (Perry, B 2021 What Happened to You? Conversations on Trauma, Resilience and Healing).

Common themes emerge and whether people are dealing with loss, adversity, bereavement or trauma they need support and connection. People will have their own individual coping mechanisms. Everyone has their own individual preferences as to how to deal with adversities. Some people will lean into exercise, talking with others, reading or listening to music. Support from others and a listening ear are usually welcome when people have the capacity for this. Giving the person an option as to whether they would like to speak about the situation or not can be very helpful. Active listening as opposed to listening to respond is of benefit to the person going through difficulty.

Mental toughness can play a vital role in the bereavement process for both adults and children. The most obvious of the eight factors of mental toughness relating to loss and bereavement is emotional control. One of the things that makes loss such a difficult thing is the myriad of emotions that someone may experience. Often, these feelings and emotions are overwhelming, simply because of how extreme and rare they are. For children, this may mean that they find it difficult or even impossible to put a name to those feelings. The important thing to remember is that all these emotions are real and valid.

However, what we do not want is for those feelings to become out of our control. Emotional control can enable a person to experience emotions and control them without letting emotions overtake them. Yes, you are allowed to be angry and upset, or feel indifferent, numb, sluggish, even helpless, but feel all those things on your own terms. Feel it to heal it. Emotions are energy in motion and they will come and go and change. Sadness is a natural response to loss and a healthy expression of this. Tears can aid the healing process.

When a child seems to be lacking in response or doesn't show emotions, ask them if they have understood what you have told them. Give them some time to process the information and revisit the subject later on. Let them know that whatever they are feeling is okay – whether it be sadness, anger, numbness, etc. - and that you feel these things too. It may help to let a child visualise their emotions through play or art.

Sometimes we are caught off guard by positive emotions. We may feel guilty of laughing, smiling or having a good time. It takes courage to allow ourselves to feel these positive feelings. Sadness can be a safe space when dealing with a loss. It is the emotion we associate most with grief, right? It is important to remember that you are allowed to be happy, even in times of grief. Being positive can help us cope with loss. Someone with higher levels of risk orientation may be more inclined to give in to these positive feelings and allow themselves to experience happiness. We will range on the scale from mentally sensitive to mentally tough and this will vary in response to big life events and challenges.

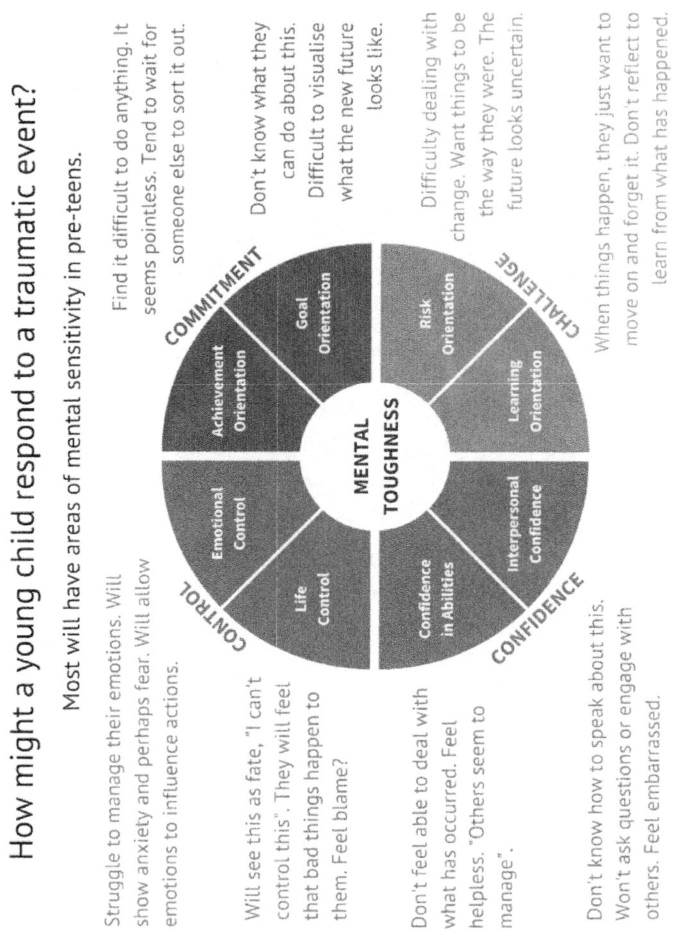

How might a young child respond to a traumatic event?

Most will have areas of mental sensitivity in pre-teens.

Commitment

- Goal Orientation: Don't know what they can do about this. Difficulty to visualise what the new future looks like.
- Achievement Orientation: Find it difficult to do anything. It seems pointless. Tend to wait for someone else to sort it out.

Challenge

- Risk Orientation: Difficulty dealing with change. Want things to be the way they were. The future looks uncertain.
- Learning Orientation: When things happen, they just want to move on and forget it. Don't reflect to learn from what has happened.

Control

- Emotional Control: Struggle to manage their emotions. Will show anxiety and perhaps fear. Will allow emotions to influence actions.
- Life Control: Will see this as fate, "I can't control this". They will feel that bad things happen to them. Feel blame?

Confidence

- Confidence in Abilities: Don't feel able to deal with what has occurred. Feel helpless. "Others seem to manage".
- Interpersonal Confidence: Don't know how to speak about this. Won't ask questions or engage with others. Feel embarrassed.

Fig. 5: Response to traumatic events

Parents' own awareness of their own strengths and weaknesses will be of benefit to themselves and their children. Self-awareness is a major issue here. If we understand our different levels of mental toughness on each factor, we are much better able to respond appropriately to events, especially in front of others.

Practising self-care and looking after yourself first can be a challenge. It is a journey but a worthwhile venture. Children learn so much from their parents through verbal and non-verbal language. You are their greatest role model which is a huge privilege but also comes with responsibility. Confidence can be shaken by grief, loss, adversity and trauma. Choosing small practical goals can help. Small tasks such as making the bed or dinner can be a challenge. The smaller steps we can take to do things that make us feel better will lead to more confidence.

Mental toughness can support us in figuring out where our baseline is on the scale from mentally sensitive to mentally tough. If we use these tools non-judgementally towards ourselves and our children, we are setting them up to see that we have agency over our lives and decisions. Some things are and always will be out of our control. Other factors are within our control and can be worked on.

Ultimately, what is important, is that the child feels comfortable confiding in others and asking them for help, as this may help them cope better. Children with higher levels of interpersonal confidence are more likely to do so. When we build strong, supportive relationships in good times, these can impact positively on how we deal with challenging situations.

The grief of having lost someone important may never be completely gone, but you can reach a point where it is manageable and on your own terms. You may be able to store the grief for and the memories of your loved one in a little box in your heart that you can open and shut when you choose to do so. This is what we want to teach our children – that they feel in control of whatever comes their way and that they feel empowered to cope with it.

9 SELF-REGULATION, CO-REGULATION VS CO-ESCALATION (SELF-AWARENESS)

Maria Lawless

Self-regulation is the ability to manage our behaviour, reactions and emotions. Self-regulation is necessary for our emotional well-being. We all face challenges and adversities in life. How we react to them is what is important.

The eight factors that make up a person's Mental Toughness are explained in further detail previously in the book (Chapter 1). There is overlap within the factors and being self-regulated allows us to make clearer decisions that support our well-being and us.

Self-regulation is vital for children and adults equally. Children learn more from how we act and behave than from what we say. Significant adults such as parents, grandparents, guardians, aunts, uncles, teachers and coaches are role models for children, teenagers and young adults. Reflecting on what tools we need when we feel tired, hungry or upset is helpful. This will be different for everyone. This is a key issue in the mental toughness concept - our mental responses are unique to each of us. Self-awareness about this means that we can identify solutions, which can work for me. One size has never fit all.

"Behaviourally, self-regulation is the ability to act in your long-term best interest, consistent with your deepest values. Emotionally, self-regulation is the ability to calm yourself down when you're upset and cheer yourself up when you're down." (Stosny, 2011) 'Psychology Today: Self-Regulation. To feel better focus on what is more important.' https://www.psychologytoday.com/ie/blog/anger-in-the-age-entitlement/201110/self-regulation. We can make better decisions when we are calm. All emotions do serve a purpose.

They are energy in motion. Anger is usually a secondary emotion. Many people are uncomfortable with anger, usually sadness or someone crossing a line can be behind anger.

Anger can be a particularly useful emotion. When it is channelled and worked through, it can cause people to act and make changes or place limits to ensure someone does not cross that line of what the individual feels is acceptable or unacceptable.

Children learn to self-regulate from co-regulation. Co-regulation begins in utero when the mother is pregnant. How regulated or dysregulated the mother is during pregnancy affects the baby. Co-regulation occurs when an adult can remain in a calm state when a child or another person has become upset, distressed or dysregulated. The child's nervous system is distressed and needs a calm other with whom they have a warm relationship with to help soothe them and their nervous system.

Co-regulation can occur through touch, a hug, breathing exercises, play, dancing, running, and movement. The biggest factor is that there is a trusted adult who in the moment may feel under pressure but can self-regulate and support the child through their challenge. When the child feels seen, heard and accepted through co-regulation they will calm and this will help them learn how to self-regulate. Co-regulation is a necessary skill throughout all aspects of our lives from childhood to adulthood. Humans are wired for connection and adults often need another to support them to co-regulate.

"A regulated, calm adult can regulate a dysregulated, anxious child but a dysregulated adult can never calm a dysregulated child" (Dr Bruce Perry. https://www.neurosequential.com/). Awareness of your own nervous system, feelings and how to self-regulate yourself is vital to ensure that you can provide a safe secure base to support your child in working through big emotions. If a dysregulated adult tries to co-regulate with a distressed child this, will heighten the situation and lead to co-escalation. This is challenging for parents and guardians as they can often become upset when their child is distressed and have many of their own challenges to deal with.

Providing a safe and secure environment for children is necessary for co-regulation. Clear and predictable routines, expectations, consequences and boundaries will enhance co-regulation. Attuning to your child occurs when a warm relationship with care and affection is provided. Responding to cues that signal needs and wants and providing support in stressful times is a key factor in self-regulation.

Boundaries mean placing limits where necessary. Children and young people can often feel like they are always being told what to do. Often this can be true. When working with children and placing boundaries I think it is often helpful to get them to help you with this. This is age-dependent and can work well with children from the ages of five upwards. Try to keep the language positive 'Please walk is more effective than don't run'. If you explain that there is not enough space, there are hazards, or moving cars and their safety is important to you. 'Please walk as cars are moving' is more effective than 'Don't run or you will hurt yourself'.

Children naturally have a strong sense of justice and like to feel that things are fair. This method keeps language and mindset positive. It also makes it clear that the desired behaviour is 'walking' as opposed to the undesired behaviour of 'running'.

Younger children may only be able to follow simple instructions so if we name the undesirable behaviour in a negative way that might be the only thing they remember and they may think of behaving in a way they would not have because an adult has highlighted it. It is like being told not to push the red button or think about an elephant.

Consistency with boundaries and consequences is the key. Children and young adults like routine, limits and boundaries. There is so much out of their control that knowing where their parent's and guardian's limits are provides a sense of safety.

Many parents and guardians can struggle with consistency and a shared co-parenting approach. Devising a contract with the children and young adults and agreeing on fair consequences can work really well. When parents and guardians can give themselves a minute to pause when the going gets tough this is of huge benefit to everyone. Consequences can still be placed but you will be less reactive and the environment will be less stormy.

Children and young people will push boundaries. That is one of their jobs. If bedtime were a struggle, it would be helpful to have a discussion and identify the obstacle. Try unwinding a little earlier and have some time for connection like a story read. If the challenge persists, an earlier bedtime might be a reasonable and helpful consequence or turning the TV off an hour earlier.

"When their storm meets our calm co-regulation occurs." (Kristin Wiens, https://self-reg.ca/co-regulation-graphic/). Their storm may not always look like that to an adult. We have learned to deal with many common crises but may have forgotten that once we were like them. When we notice frustrations or distress in our children whatever way they present them, we can take this as an opportunity to co-regulate and connect with them.

Teaching and coaching self-regulation skills to children is a worthwhile process. We can do this by using and verbalising our own self-regulation techniques. This will provide children opportunities to use the skills and co-regulate with a caregiver.

Co-regulation is the art of first regulating ourselves, and then creating a safe space for children to co-regulate. When you fly on an aeroplane, the emergency advice is always to put on your own oxygen mask first. Co-regulation is similar in that self-regulation must come first. You cannot calm a distressed child if you are also distressed.

Young children's brains and their pre-frontal cortex have not fully developed. The pre-frontal cortex controls emotions, logic, and reasoning and regulation skills. Has anyone ever told you to calm down when you are feeling stressed and dysregulated? Has this ever succeeded in calming you down? In my experience, this works zero per cent of the time. If this does not work for adults, we should reflect and not expect it to work for children either.

We need to identify and reflect on what works for our own self-regulation. There are three main states of physiological arousal. We feel these states within our bodies. These are hypo-arousal, optimal state of arousal and hyper-arousal.

Hypo-arousal can present as a freeze response, it can occur when people are feeling tired, sluggish, apathetic, overwhelmed, emotionally numb, paralyzed or burnt out. Hyper-arousal is the fight or flight response and can present as hypervigilance, a feeling of anxiety and panic, mind racing, excessive energy, frustration and anger. The optimal state of arousal is when we feel regulated, and content and our needs are met.

We will all move through the various states of arousal. External events and stresses will contribute to our states of arousal at different times. We cannot set up camp and live in any one state of arousal indefinitely. The trick for us as adults is to reflect on where we are. Upon reflection, we can identify our needs to move forward or back to the optimal state of arousal.

Dr Dan Siegel talks about our 'window of tolerance' (Siegel &

Bryson, 2011). When a person is in their optimal state of arousal or window of tolerance, it is generally the case "that the brain is functioning well and can effectively process what happens to us and around us. The individual is likely able to reflect, think rationally, and make decisions calmly without feeling either overwhelmed or withdrawn".

When a person is in a hypo or hyper state of arousal, they are outside their window of tolerance. This means that they may be unable to process information effectively. The pre-frontal cortex part of the brain, which controls emotions, logic and reasoning, has shut down. This leads to dysregulation and affects the ability to think rationally.

When faced with not being able to reason and regulate; the ability to make decisions beneficial to us is missing in action. This can lead to a person being withdrawn or over-reactive. Traumatic experiences or adversities and challenges can lead to a person being pushed out of their window of tolerance.

Co-escalation is the opposite of co-regulation. Co-escalation occurs when a child and adult are both dysregulated. Our nervous systems are heightened; there is no sense of calm. Both parties are reactive.

Our nervous systems act like a mirror to each other. It can be difficult to remain calm in the face of challenging behaviour. If we react, we risk making the situation worse and rupturing the relationship. Challenging behaviour can be addressed after co-regulation. We need the brain to move from fight or flight mode to rest and digest to access logic and reasoning.

We can think about our states of arousal like a speedometer on a car. The Alert program uses this concept with children to encourage and develop body awareness. (https://www.alertprogram.com/). Children are asked 'How is your engine running'? This is a good exercise for adults to use to identify which stage of arousal they are in and what they need.

On the left-hand side we use a blue colour to represent a hypo state of arousal, green is in the middle for the optimal state of arousal and red is to the right for the hyper state of arousal. There will be common themes for children, parents and guardians about what they need to move from one state of arousal to another but there will be individual differences. Connection will be an important need for children in all states.

Some people need connection in a hypo state of arousal whereas others may need a few minutes alone. An awareness of our own needs and our co-parent's needs in various states will aid a smoother journey to the optimal state of arousal. Nature, meditation, breathing exercises, movement, dance and music are all of benefit and are helpful healthy coping mechanisms.

Different coping mechanisms will appeal to different individuals. Certain techniques and tools may be of more benefit in certain states. Some individuals may favour breathing exercises when in a hyper state of arousal and others may favour movement or nature. The toolkit will contain common themes. Individuals through trial and error and previous experience will see which fits them best to support their level of mental toughness.

When we manage to self-regulate, we are creating a safe space and modelling self-regulation practices for children. This provides an ideal environment for co-regulation. "Adults have to be able to create a sanctuary of safety and connection so children and youth can feel their way into a space where they feel that safety" (Desautels, 2020). Co-regulation is about developing awareness with the child. It is helping them walk through the storm as opposed to trying to avoid the storm.

Our nervous system and their nervous system react to each other. We can influence our own nervous system through breathing, checking our body language and using a soothing tone of voice. This signals to our children that we are a safe space and can hold space for any emotions and behaviours that they may need to externalise safely.

The core attitude of emotional control is 'I am able to manage my emotions when under pressure and act rationally'. When we are in our window of tolerance and self-regulated, we feel this attitude and sense of emotional control. This is being able to manage our emotions; noticing them, feeling them and working through them as opposed to our emotions taking over and managing us.

Through modelling, mentoring and coaching our children with them seeing us in this regulated state then we can co-regulate. From this, children learn how to do the same and feel a sense of emotional control in their own lives.

The core attitude of life control is 'I have a sense of self-worth and I feel in enough control of my life to succeed'. Self-regulation is a form of self-care as the saying goes 'you can't pour from an empty cup'. Through the practice of self-regulation and co-regulation, you are creating space for yourself, nourishing your nervous system and your child's nervous system. This leads to a sense of self-worth and provides confidence through practice that you and your child can make better decisions and have real influence over your own life.

The core attitude of confidence in abilities is 'I have self-belief in my abilities to deal with whatever happens and will use those abilities'. Mental toughness is a spectrum from mentally tough to mentally sensitive. Self-regulation is also a spectrum and our windows of tolerance will change based on challenges experienced. There is an obvious link between mental toughness and the power to self-regulate through practice.

Confidence in abilities and self-belief can be nurtured, through realising the power of our own abilities to influence our sense of well-being. Knowing that we have previously come through challenges and can find our way out of these through our own tool kit will enhance confidence.

Interpersonal confidence is the core belief that 'I can influence and engage with others productively'. Co-regulation is a team sport and requires two people, generally an adult and a child. When co-regulation occurs, it provides a safe space and a sense of calm and well-being for both parties. Co-regulation in itself reinforces the Mental Toughness concept that 'I can influence and engage with others productively' as this is exactly what it does for both parties.

Achievement orientation is the core belief that 'I am prepared to work hard and do what it takes to succeed. I am not easily distracted. Co-regulation can be hard work at times and when we are feeling dysregulated; our ability to focus is greatly impaired. Through successful co-regulation practices, achievement orientation can be reached and our ability to focus enhanced.

Goal orientation is the core attitude that 'I set goals and targets for important things in my life. These motivate me. I have a purpose. There is a good reason for me having to do this.'

Goals only really work if they are linked to purpose. When we are in our optimal state of arousal then our brain and pre-frontal cortex are working to their highest ability. This state is the optimal state for goal setting and reflecting on and identifying the important things in our lives. Self-regulation and co-regulation allow our brains and ourselves to reach our optimal potential.

Risk orientation is the core attitude that 'I am open to change, to new experiences and to opportunity. Change does not frighten me'. When we feel fear, our brain is in fight or flight mode and only the amygdala is in working order. The amygdala is the survival alarm system in our brain to warn us of threats whether real or perceived threat.

The amygdala is a very useful tool for us and if we are being chased by a tiger, we do not need access to all parts of our brain. We need to think quickly to escape, our body is flooded with the stress hormone cortisol and we get an adrenal rush. In modern-day society, the threat of being chased by a tiger would be highly unlikely. Our amygdala scans our environment for threats regardless.

When we feel fear, we are dysregulated and, in a hypo, or hyper state of arousal. Taking risks would be the last thing on our minds, as we would not feel safe enough to deal with this. Self and co-regulation allow us to feel safe within our own nervous systems and bodies and with another. Only when one is in this state can we then embrace the Mental Toughness concept of risk orientation and step out of our comfort zones.

Learning orientation is the core attitude that 'I reflect and learn from all I experience and see –even setbacks. I focus on solutions. There will be times when we will have challenges regulating emotions and ourselves. In turn, this will be a challenge to co-regulate, as we will have to reach an optimal state of arousal to do this successfully.

We are only human and life throws up all kinds of challenges and adversities for us all. Through trial and error and identifying what works for us in our tool kit on a given day, we can permit ourselves to make mistakes. If we can be compassionate and gentle with ourselves until we feel a little better then we can reflect and learn what worked one day, why it did not another day.

There is a huge link between compassion and self-awareness. When you become aware of your thoughts and your self-talk or language that you use to yourself this can become an invaluable tool. Often, we can be very hard on ourselves and sometimes we can speak to ourselves in less than positive terms. It can be helpful to pause, take a step back and think what would I say to a good friend. If someone I loved spoke to me like this, would I be okay with it? If not, why am I speaking to myself in this way?

The longest relationship we will ever have is with ourselves. Often parents and guardians will say 'I do everything for everyone else first and put myself last'. This is the reality in many houses. On an aeroplane, the safety advice is to place your own oxygen mask on first. You need to look after yourself before you can look after others.

Children and young adults are like sponges soaking up everything we do and speak. They will hear how you speak to yourself and they will learn from you. If you find it difficult to be kind to yourself for yourself, do it for the children. You want the best for your child and you want them to have a healthy relationship and positive talk to themselves. You are their greatest teacher, which is a huge privilege and responsibility all in one. This is a lifelong journey so do not feel under pressure to do it all at once. Take it one step at a time and give yourself the same respect and compassion you give to others.

Were any of our basic human needs not met that day? Were we hungry or were we sleep deprived? This allows us flexibility with ourselves and space for curiosity and it models for children that setbacks are common and will happen but so is overcoming obstacles.

Jigsaw is an Irish charity that supports young people's mental health. They have done a lot of research on the importance of One Good Adult in a child's life. Young people who have one good adult tend to have "increased self-esteem, more success in school life, better mental health, more likely to seek help and less risk-taking behaviours.

Not having One Good Adult is linked to higher levels of distress, anti-social behaviour and increased risk for suicidal behaviour. One Good Adult is crucial to helping young people do well and to flourish" (Jigsaw, https://jigsaw.ie).

Awareness is key to mental toughness, self-regulation and co-regulation. Reflecting on small wins when we were calm and fully able to support ourselves and our child can be of huge benefit. What supported us to be able to be in this optimal state on that day? Reflecting on the more challenging days and what may have been an obstacle for us to remain calm on the given day can also be of benefit.

Asking yourself questions such as; How do I manage my emotions? What works for me? Will this work for my child? How can I connect with them? Can I take five to ten minutes for uninterrupted playtime and connection with my child? How can I support myself to deal with challenges in a more helpful way? What does showing up for myself look like? The answers may look and be different on different days depending on external demands and needs. It is a process but one that will nurture self-awareness and mental toughness.

10 PUTTING THINGS INTO CONTEXT

In previous chapters, we have presented what mental toughness is, why it is important as well as the most common concerns and issues reported by parents and how the mental toughness of the parent and child plays a role in this. Throughout this, we have pointed to development suggestions.

In the next five chapters, we will delve into further detail on their principles of mental toughness development and how to support your child's mental toughness through a range of practical activities.

11 THE IMPORTANCE OF DEVELOPING MENTAL TOUGHNESS

Oktawia Hryp-Czerwińska

Developing mental toughness in children is particularly important in the context of shaping their start into adulthood. Among adults, there is a common belief "Let the children be children", which is intended to emphasise the fact that children have natural cognitive abilities that are quite sufficient to develop appropriately.

As it was written in Chapter 2 - we learn most things by experience, so at some point, it might be true. Indeed, let children be children, but remember that for the kids who are currently a few years old, it will only take 14-15 years to enter adulthood. Is that a lot? Yes and no...

It is definitely not a long time because even when our children start their studies at university or start their first job, we still think that they are only our children and we hope that we have done everything for them to deal with these events as best as they can.

However, this is enough time for us as parents, guardians or teachers to accept the task of "preparing children for adult life". Usually, during this time we devote ourselves to ensuring that our children enter adulthood with the widest possible knowledge and as many skills as possible.

The so-called "good start" is associated strictly with having competencies, or sometimes already at this stage qualifications in a specific field, for example, sports. For many years, this approach was sufficient. Gaining good academic or professional qualifications would be seen as the factor that would set you up for life.

However, the changing world requires something more from us. It demands more from us adults now, and it will be even more demanding, as time goes on, for the generations that are now being born.

Therefore, it is worth focusing not only on providing them with the best education, and hours spent on extracurricular activities or additional courses but also to take great care of mental preparation for adult life and new roles. Employers are already paying more and more attention to non-competency elements sometimes collected together and described under the term "a good attitude" - particular attention is paid to aspects such as self-confidence, confidence in abilities, goal orientation, control of emotions and development orientation. Sounds familiar? Yes, these are the areas that mental toughness covers!

To better understand why mental toughness is so important, it is worth reaching for concepts that describe the current world. Mainly these concepts are used to describe the business world. Although it may not seem to be our concern, it affects each of us in some indirect way. Awareness of these concepts allows you to better understand what is happening in the world around us and gives you a chance to adapt accordingly not only with your skills but also with your attitudes. The world is becoming more and more difficult to understand and navigate, which is why it is in our hands to properly prepare children mentally.

So far it has been said that we live in a VUCA world.

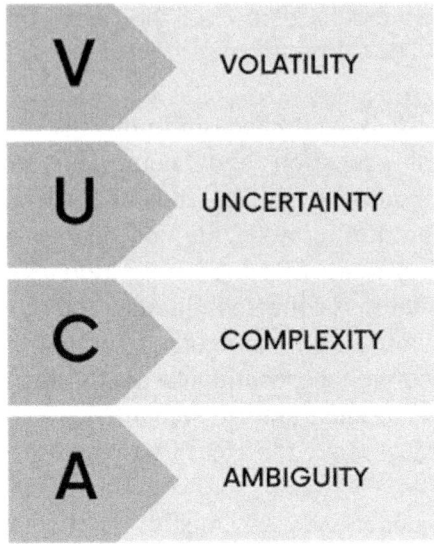

Fig. 6: VUCA

The acronym VUCA was originally described in 1985 by two economists, Warren Bennis and Burt Dwarf, who conducted considerations on leadership styles. Then, in the late 1980s and early 1990s, the United States Army War College used the concept to describe the state of the post-Cold War world.

However, the peak popularisation of this concept fell in the first decade of the 21st century, when many fields of science, such as psychology, sociology and economics, began to use them to explain what was happening.

At that time, many discussions were started on how the definition of the VUCA world can help us persevere in it and at the same time fulfil ourselves in the professional sphere. In principle, until recently, the concept of VUCA seemed to be adequate to the global situation all the time, and subsequent considerations only led to the creation of new ways of adapting.

And then, in 2020, there comes an article written by Jamais Cascio, an American anthropologist, historian and futurist. In his article, he points to the fact that the concept of VUCA and its definition, for sure, explains to us in a very simple but concise way the world we live in and how we should function in it, but there is no perspective for the future, and it is crucial in this way we will prepare ourselves for what's to come. As a supplement to the VUCA concept, Jamais Cascio points to the BANI concept.

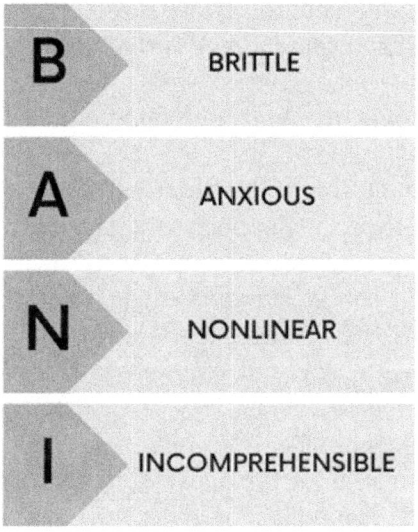

Fig. 7: BANI

The concept of the BANI world describes not so much what is now, but what we can expect. The world in which we will have to function (and above all in which nowadays children will enter their adulthood) is a fragile, anxious, non-linear world that is difficult to understand and incomprehensible.

The explanation for the "BANI" acronym may cause concern itself. While the explanation of the VUCA acronym was also not very optimistic at first glance, the volatility, complexity or ambiguity could also be seen as changes, chances and new opportunities. The concept of BANI, however, is not intended to scare us and fill us with anxiety, but to show what we should prepare our children for, and of course also ourselves.

The concept of BANI gained great publicity very quickly. As in the case of VUCA, more and more ideas and answers to the question appear over time: "Okay, we already know what to expect. So how do you prepare for it?". Although there is no clear recipe for how to deal with life, the idea of mental toughness is gaining more and more importance in this context. What should be understood and kept in mind is that mental toughness allows us to react most adequately to events in our lives and go through them without much of a mark on our mental health.

In the coming times, it will be extremely important for our children, and especially important to show resilience in aspects such as a sense of control over their own lives, control of emotions, self-confidence and their own skills, as well as learning through their own experiences - they are the ones that significantly will allow our children to face the challenges of BANI world.

The confirmation of the above statements is also the report of the World Economic Forum - New Vision for Education: Fostering Social and Emotional Learning through Technology, published in 2016). It is also commonly said that the labour market will undergo huge changes in the next 20 years. It is expected that some professions may disappear completely or undergo thorough redefinition. Estimated that in 10 years 40% of the jobs that exist now won't exist. And that of the jobs that will exist, 40% don't yet exist. How can you plan for a future like this?

One of the few things that awaits our children is uncertainty and fragility. The World Economic Forum (WEF) organisation, however, indicates in its report the key skills of the 21st century - the absolute essence of what young people should be familiar with in the education system, and what features they should have developed to enter adult professional life without significant obstacles.

What catches the eye at the first review is a clear division into three categories: foundational literacies, competencies and, most importantly, in the context of the development of mental toughness, strategic character qualities are also indicated. This shows us how much the understanding of human capital has changed in recent years – it is no longer just about hard skills, but to a large extent we also look at behaviours, attitudes and the way of reacting in specific situations.

Below you can see the absolutely basic skills that WEF identifies as crucial for students in the 21st century.

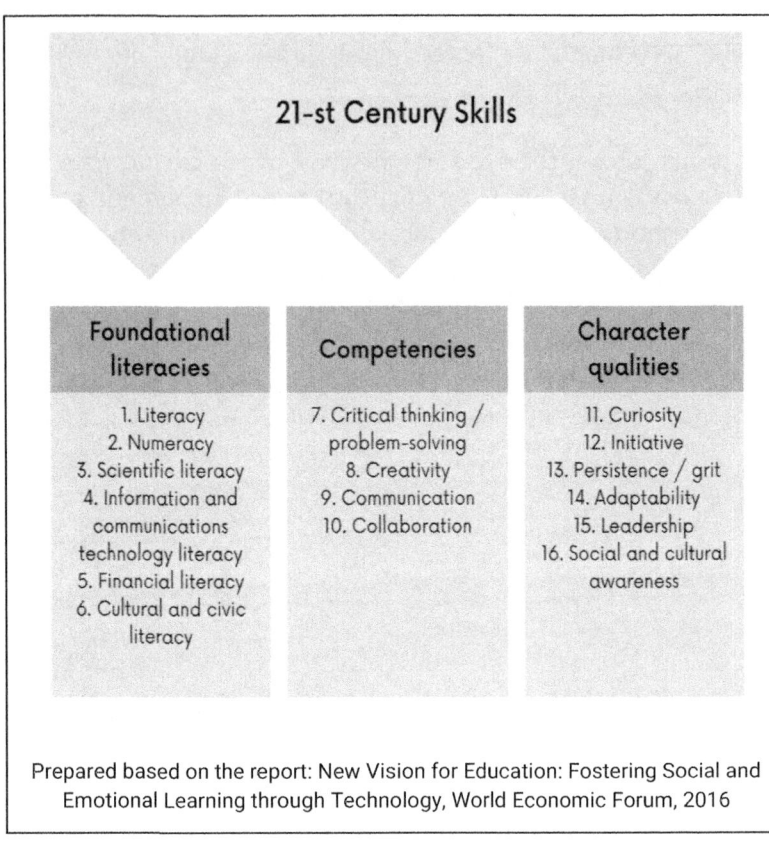

Fig. 8: Skills for the 21st Century

Mental toughness itself, as a reminder, is a personality trait, which means that it greatly influences how we deal with specific situations. A character trait (like those indicated above) is something that we can develop, and using it in practice largely depends on our personality. Therefore, by working on mental toughness in specific scales, we have a chance to influence which character traits we will use fluently. Most of these character traits fit perfectly with the definitions provided in the model of mental toughness. The justification for each of these associations results directly from the behaviours and attitudes described in the research on the tool for measuring mental toughness.

Skill	Corresponding areas from the model of mental toughness	Justification
Character		
Curiosity	Risk orientation, learning orientation	One has to agree that there is no curiosity without learning orientation and a willingness to take risks. People who score higher on the challenge scale are curious about the world and thus engage with new projects and activities.
Initiative	Learning orientation, confidence in abilities, interpersonal confidence	Components conducive to taking initiative can undoubtedly include such elements as faith in one's own skills and self-confidence in interpersonal relations – rarely do people without these features take initiative. In people with high scores in the above areas, taking initiative is one of the guiding motives of their actions.
Persistence	Achievement orientation, goal orientation, confidence in	Persistence is what keeps us on course despite the difficulties we encounter along the way. Therefore, developing resilience in the area of

	abilities, life control, and emotional control.	achieving results and being goal-oriented seems to be crucial for this character trait to become our strength. Believing in one's own abilities allows for a clear look at the situation and the choice of skills that will be necessary to overcome difficulties. Feeling in control of our lives will eliminate the feeling that something just happens to us and will add faith that we are in charge of our lives. Emotional control, on the other hand, will allow you to react appropriately when difficulties arise.
Adaptability	The whole mental toughness model	You could say that the whole idea of resilience is, in a way, necessary to talk about adaptability - we definitely need emotional control. Confidence in one's skills also seems to be extremely useful here, because then we can consciously use exactly those we need at a specific moment. The scale of challenges and showing resilience within them will allow you to take risks and gain experience from experiences.

Table 2 Character traits and mental toughness

When it comes to competencies, it should be remembered that competencies consist of knowledge, skills and attitude. In some sources, attitude is replaced by social competence, which supports the constant and proficient application of knowledge and skills in practice. Therefore, in this case, as part of the description, we will focus on showing how mental toughness interacts with the attitudes of individual competencies indicated by the WEF.

Competence		
Critical thinking / problem-solving	Emotional control, risk orientation, goal orientation	According to the definition, critical thinking is a kind of realistic thinking, focused on making an appraisal of what we encounter. Therefore, it should be taken into account that the effect of this way of thinking may be various conclusions that we have to face. We must be willing to take the risk of formulating appropriate conclusions, then be able to control the accompanying emotions and, consequently, solve the problem, it is worth showing an attitude focused on achieving goals.
Creativity	Learning orientation	It should be remembered that creativity is not only innovation and creating something completely new but also finding connections between what we already know to better understand or create a completely new point of view. It is difficult if we are unable to draw lessons from experience and do not crave new knowledge.
Communication	Emotional control, confidence in abilities, interpersonal confidence	In interpersonal communication, we need the ability to control emotions, but it is worth pointing out here that people with high scores on the "confidence" scale can communicate much better because they are sure of their opinions, and they can manifest confidence in their skills, knowledge and opinions. In

		addition, self-confidence in interpersonal relationships helps to cope with the challenges we encounter in communication with other people - for example, confrontation or differences in communication styles.
Collaboration	Emotional control, confidence in abilities, interpersonal confidence, goal orientation, and learning orientation.	Effective and fruitful cooperation requires many attitudes and behaviours on the part of each team member. Control of emotions allows you to behave appropriately in the event of a difference of opinion or difficulties, for example on the way to the implementation of a project. Confidence in one's own skills and self-confidence in interpersonal relations allows for a free exchange of opinions, with an emphasis on direct communication of one's point of view. Goal orientation allows us to focus on the team task to be performed, as well as on delivering the part that we participate in teamwork. Orientation to learning, or learning from one's own experiences, allows for reflection, which in turn allows for using this in every subsequent team cooperation.

Table 3 *Competencies and mental toughness*

To summarise, the future of our children and their entry into adulthood will be ruled by a completely different reality than those we know as parents, guardians and teachers. The extent to which knowledge about our personalities, psyche and mental health has developed should be the starting point in considering how to prepare children to enter adult life and go through the stage of early adulthood.

Generational changes, the global economic situation, as well as other significant events in the world have a huge impact on what young people will face in a dozen or so years, on the verge of adulthood, their first professional commitments and choosing their life path.

All of this has sparked a heated, but very important, discussion around the world about how our children are doing in today's world and what we owe them as adults responsible for them. Technological proficiency and very early access to information make acquiring skills much easier for current and future generations than for us, adults, who are already mature at this point.

What, however, is still missing as a permanent element of education systems, as well as social policies in many countries, is the care for the psychological and mental sphere of children's development. Self-awareness and the development of mental toughness are therefore undoubtedly something that seems to be necessary and a priority when we think about the future of our children.

12 CULTIVATING MENTAL TOUGHNESS IN CHILDREN – EMPOWERING STRATEGIES FOR PARENTS

Kasia Więckowska

Our world today is full of challenges, uncertainties, stressors and pressure as well as opportunities. This applies not only to adults but also to younger children who face adversities and difficult situations in their lives.

More than ever mental toughness has become an increasingly valuable asset worth developing in young people. Mental toughness equips individuals with the courage, determination and adaptability needed to navigate obstacles and thrive in life.

As a parent, one of the greatest gifts you can offer to your child is the possibility to develop a resilient and positive attitude to everything they encounter – we call this mental toughness. As parents, you play the role of teacher, coach, mentor and role model all rolled into one.

Children observe and copy their parents in many ways. Why not focus this on instilling and developing important qualities in your whole family, including you as a parent with your child?

Mental toughness can be developed, similarly to emotional intelligence, perseverance, grit or optimism. As a parent, you play a vital role in helping children build the foundation for this lifelong mindset and attitude – their mental toughness.

However, before we equip you with strategies, let us, first, introduce you to a basic knowledge of child brain development. Understanding brain plasticity – the natural ability of the brain to change and adapt throughout life, as well as brain development can empower you as a parent in your efforts to cultivate mental toughness in your child. This information can provide you with valuable insights into how mental toughness can be fostered in children.

During childhood and adolescence, the human brain undergoes significant changes, particularly in areas responsible for executive functions, decision-making, emotional regulation or speech and the creation of social bonds. Knowing this as a parent can help you to create an environment that stimulates positive brain development and supports the development of mental toughness.

Growth mindset is a popular concept that appears to be connected with this idea of brain plasticity. Usefully the mental toughness concept embraces the idea of a growth mindset adding a detailed explanation of how this has several factors or components.

When a child believes that abilities and intelligence can be developed through effort, exercise and practising, it is more likely they will engage in challenging activities that promote brain growth. It is important to help a child understand that intelligence is not fixed, but with practice and perseverance, it can be enhanced. Parents have a great power to foster an approach that supports mental toughness.

Stress is not the best friend for a child's developing brain. Experiencing manageable levels of stress can actually strengthen neural circuits associated with coping and adaptability. However, on the other end, chronic or overwhelming stress can impair brain development.

Given that a child's brain is not yet fully developed, this is why they really need their parent's support in managing stress and regulating emotions effectively. Self-regulation which is explained below and explored in more detail earlier in chapter 9, is a crucial skill your child can learn from you and with a parent's careful support and guidance.

Spending time with your children might be crucial for your child's mental toughness growth as well as for positive brain development. Engaging with children in activities that promote cognitive development and executive functions is great fun and activities such as Puzzles, problem-solving tasks and strategic games help strengthen neural connections and enhance critical thinking skills.

In addition, activities that require self-control and delayed gratification, as well as setting and achieving goals, support the development of mental toughness by strengthening the prefrontal cortex, the brain region responsible for self-regulation, problem-solving, decision making or moderating social behaviour.

Physical exercise also provides significant benefits for brain development and mental toughness development. Research has shown that regular physical activity increases blood flow to the brain, releases stress, enhances the production of neurotransmitters and promotes the growth of new neurons, improving cognitive abilities and emotional resilience.

At birth, the child's brain is not fully developed, in general, it still needs around 25 years to be fully formed. Parents have an incredible opportunity here. Experiences and behaviours can shape neural pathways and strengthen connections in the brain and mental toughness can be developed through intentional and repeated practice of skills and strategies.

In this section, you will find practical strategies that a parent can employ to support your child's mental toughness and empower them to manage life's hurdles and succeed in life.

Choose the best strategies that will support you and get creative. Each child is an individual, each human being is different and special. The remainder of this chapter explores strategies for developing those components of the mental toughness framework already described in earlier chapters.

More specific tools and techniques are provided at the end of this book.

The **Control** aspect describes the extent to which I believe I can shape and influence my life, and what is happening around me, that I can make a difference and achieve what is necessary.

Life Control	I think I am worthwhile - I will "give most things a go".
Emotional Control	I can manage my emotions and make good decisions.

Promote Emotional Intelligence - Understanding and managing own emotions as well as empathizing with others plays a crucial role in child development. These are skills you as a parent can show to your child daily and they can learn by observing you in many social circumstances.

Emotional intelligence can be developed by encouraging open communication at home, together with active listening, validating and discussing feelings and emotions. Naming emotions is a skill that can be developed through books, games or social role-playing at home or school. Cooperating and playing with groups of other children can be one of the best daily exercises you can encourage in your children.

Teach your children how to recognise and regulate emotions, resolve conflicts peacefully and show compassion towards others. Be a role model for your child, teach by example and not only why what you say should be done.

As the skills grow your child will be well-adjusted to navigate into strong and healthy social interactions with others.

Mindfulness helps build self-awareness - Introducing mindfulness practices to children has shown benefits in reducing stress, enhancing emotional regulation and improving focus.

Encouraging just simple mindfulness exercises such as deep breathing or listening exercises can support your child to calm down and reduce stress or anger.

You can introduce a game to see who is the quickest to identify and calm down difficult emotions in your family. There is a powerful breathing exercise suggested in many books – let your child imagine a flower in one hand and a candle in the other. You breathe in and smell the imaginary flower and breathe out to blow out an imaginary candle.

This is great fun for the whole family and those observing as well. Through using fun and mindfulness exercises, you can help your child develop self-awareness and learn how to manage challenging situations by themselves.

Build a Growth-Oriented Home - Psychological studies highlight the significance of the family environment in shaping children's mental toughness. Foster an atmosphere that values effort, growth and learning.

Encourage open dialogue, problem-solving and planning discussions as well as shared decision-making to promote autonomy and significance. Bear in mind that children love to be heard. When planning vacation time, consider your child's ideas and let them choose tasks you will perform together during time off.

Sit together to plan a split of responsibilities to clean the house. Let your child make their own mistakes, and give them money so they can learn to control the budget. Give them the independence that they need to grow.

The **Commitment** aspect reflects the extent to which we make promises, to ourselves and others and the extent to which we are determined to keep those promises.

Goal Orientation	I have self-belief in my abilities to deal with things.
Achievement Orientation	I am prepared to work hard & do what it takes to succeed.

Setting Realistic Goals and Providing Support – We are not born with the ability to set goals and make plans. This is a skill that you can start to teach your children at a very young age. When clearing away toys after play, make a plan for who puts a ball and a teddy bear into a box. Support your child to take a step-by-step approach to do this - which toys, which part of the room and how they can make a difference together with you.

Help your child set realistic and achievable goals that challenge them without overwhelming them. When your child has a small project to complete, and plenty of homework to do, break larger goals into smaller, manageable steps (this approach is called "how do you eat an elephant – a slice at a time").

Celebrate progress, be excited, and offer support, guidance and encouragement where needed. Let your child work on their own with the plan created and help them understand that setbacks are a natural part of the journey.

Rewire Your Child's Brain and Help them build Motivation – Your child's brain is plastic. It is capable of change and development. This is something you can utilise at every stage of your child's development to support their mental toughness.

Rewiring your child's brain is highly influenced by parenting styles.

Children can learn best through experiences and by making mistakes. When you do everything for your child, you can take away their confidence in their abilities to do even simple things. Taking initiative and completing planned actions builds and strengthens self-confidence and a sense of self-worth.

Teach your child how to adopt the daily routine of dressing and planning their day, preparing materials for preschool, and planning homework tasks as achievable actions.

Autonomy also helps build internal motivation and supports taking on more demanding challenges. One way to develop internal motivation is to appreciate the efforts and recognise the process that leads to success, rather than solely focusing on the result and success itself. You can make a difference by just letting your child be, learn and play at their own pace, and their own way.

Bring Physical Activity to Your Life – Physical activities release tension and stress. It has also been shown that engaging in unstructured play and regular physical activity improves cognitive, emotional and behavioural skills. Spend active, family time outdoors to play, and practice sports and allow your children to explore, take risks and develop grit to complete a task despite obstacles and difficulties.

Challenge This component of mental toughness represents the aspect of how you respond to challenges, meaning activities or events that are new and out of the ordinary, which can mean we need to stretch ourselves and learn new skills to complete those activities.

Risk Orientation	I see opportunity when exposed to new situations.
Learning Orientation	I think about all that happens to me and learn from that.

Encouraging a Growth Mindset – A growth mindset is a belief that abilities and intelligence can be developed through effort, dedication and learning from mistakes. By fostering a growth mindset, you as a parent can help your child perceive challenges as opportunities for growth.

Encourage your child to view failures as stepping stones to success, emphasizing the importance of perseverance and praising effort rather than focusing solely on outcomes. Try to focus on the process of creation and not only the result.

Professor Carol S. Dweck identified that students who are praised for their effort in achieving a task are more likely to be motivated and willing to tackle more challenging tasks. On the contrary, students who were praised for the result and their intelligence were less eager and less persistent to take on more challenging tasks.

Effort-based praise is believed to promote a belief that abilities can be developed through hard work, your child might eventually love to learn new skills which will help them develop mental toughness, as trying new things builds confidence and high self-esteem.

It is important to keep this balanced. It is important to recognise effort leading to some degree of success. Simply praising effort can be counterproductive.

Allow Adversity – Resilience is the ability to bounce back from setbacks. To build that part of mental toughness provide your child with age-appropriate challenges and support them through difficult times if needed.

Encourage them and guide them to problem-solve, cope with stress and obstacles and develop healthy ways of dealing with failure. Failure is an opportunity to learn, an obstacle is an opportunity to get creative. Allow your child to face and overcome challenges to help them build self-confidence.

Encourage Healthy Risk-Taking – Taking calculated risks may help your child step out of their comfort zone allowing them personal growth. Trying new things may help your child find new passions and can encourage them to face challenges more eagerly.

Show your child how to assess risks, make decisions and learn from both success and failures. By installing a sense of adventure and the willingness to take calculated risks, you can nurture your child's mental toughness.

The fourth construct – **Confidence** – describes to what extent you believe you have the ability, knowledge, experience and skills to deal with everything that is coming into your life, how you deal with obstacles and setbacks as well as the way you respond to others when those appear.

Confidence in Abilities	I have self-belief in my abilities to deal with things.
Interpersonal Confidence	I am happy to engage with and to influence others.

The Power of Positive Reinforcement – research suggest that using positive reinforcement is more effective than punishment or criticism in promoting desirable behaviour and building mental toughness in children. Acknowledge and reward their efforts and achievements as this reinforces their motivation and self-belief. Teach your child to speak well about themselves, notice what they did well, and what they can still learn to do even better.

This is particularly important as children learn new skills.

Developing Self-Compassion – Being kind and compassionate to oneself and others builds self-confidence, raises self-esteem, and increases optimism and motivation. Teach your child to be kind and understanding towards themselves, particularly in the face of setbacks or failures.

Help them reframe negative self-talk and internal criticism and promote self-acceptance. Also, bear in mind that a child learns by observation, if you wish to wire self-compassion into your child's brain you have to show similar behaviours and attitudes first.

Strengthen Social Support and Impact – Research suggests that strong social connections contribute to mental toughness. Encouraging children to cultivate healthy relationships such as friendships and mentorships is necessary to grow socially.

Relationships provide emotional support and a sense of belonging, which is a very important need for any child. Playing and spending time in groups provide opportunities for learning from others' experiences. Interpersonal confidence is an important aspect of building mental toughness.

In summary, there is a great deal a parent can do to support the development of their child. Particularly to develop resilience and a positive approach to life, which are the cornerstones of mental toughness.

A parent, with careful thought and application, can be a teacher, coach, mentor and role model.

13 DEVELOPING MENTAL TOUGHNESS

Helen St Clair-Thompson

How can parents support the development of children's mental toughness?

In this chapter, we now focus on developing children's mental toughness. As discussed in Chapter One, mental toughness has implications for well-being, agility, aspirations, and attainment, and therefore as a parent, we may want our children to develop mental toughness.

Some children will be mentally sensitive. It is important to remember that the mentally sensitive can prosper- with self-awareness. However, all things being equal, possessing a degree of mental toughness conveys an advantage in many useful settings.

As discussed earlier in the book, research has suggested that mental toughness is at least to some extent malleable, so it can be developed given the right environment and support. As parents, we have an important role to play here, although of course teachers and peers may be important too.

The development of children's mental toughness can of course be influenced by parenting behaviours, as considered in chapter two. The aim of this chapter, though, is to consider some broad principles that may be important for mental toughness development. We will return occasionally to parenting practices but will think beyond supportive and controlling parenting behaviours.

We will describe some broad principles for developing children's mental toughness. These are based on research that has been conducted in the domain of parenting, but also in the domains of education and sport. Later in the book, we will then follow this with more detail about developing mental toughness, in the form of a toolkit.

Experiential learning

It is widely known that children need to encounter physical and mental challenges to develop resilience. Research has shown that people who experience a moderate amount of adversity are better at dealing with stress and have better well-being than people who have had no such experience, and people who have faced too much adversity. We, therefore, need to allow our children to face difficult situations (whilst also hoping they don't have to face too much adversity).

Parenting is important in terms of the extent to which children are exposed to or protected from challenges. A good example of this is what has come to be known as helicopter parenting. This is an overprotecting and controlling parenting style, with the term "helicopter parenting" describing how parents may hover over their children, ready to come to the rescue if needed in a difficult situation. Children are protected from challenges, and consequently, they do not develop resilience. Children may also come to believe that they are incapable of dealing with things themselves.

When children reach adolescence, modern technologies may allow helicopter parenting to thrive. With technology, there are several ways for parents to track their children. Using apps such as Find My iPhone, Snapchat and Life360, parents can constantly know where their children are. Life360 even allows parents to know how fast their children are driving and where they are going. Parents can also set restrictions on the content that children can access from their devices.

Many of these technologies just aim to protect children's

safety, but parents can become accustomed to knowing where their children are, who they have been with, and what they have been doing. This overprotectiveness can lead parents to think that this is the norm, and they may have the tendency to intervene in difficult situations or remove barriers for children to achieve. This can ultimately lead to parents thwarting their children's experiential learning.

Instead, parents need to allow their children to face challenges and difficult situations themselves, and this will allow them to develop mental toughness. Parents should also encourage children to reflect upon situations in which they might have been successful in doing so; providing them with confidence in their abilities and increasing the likelihood that they will be willing to undertake challenging tasks in the future.

Some would argue that in addition to allowing children to face and overcome challenges themselves, parents should actively create situations that are difficult and stressful. Here we can draw a comparison to the world of sports; coaches commonly believe that athletes should be challenged regularly to ensure that they don't settle into a comfort zone. Challenges should not be so difficult that athletes cannot complete them but should be attainable with effort and hard work. In this way, when a difficult situation arises, for example in a competition, an athlete can respond more effectively. Similarly, as parents we can set difficult tasks for our children, on which children can be successful with some effort and persistence.

Knowing your child

All children are different and will respond to events in different ways. It is important for a parent to understand how a child is likely to feel or what they may think in a situation. There are also many advantages of knowing the strengths and weaknesses that children may have and encouraging them to use or develop them.

A recent term that has appeared in the positive psychology literature is strength-based parenting. This involves recognising the strengths of a child and encouraging them to use these strengths. The first thing that is important here is strengths knowledge; having an accurate understanding of a child's strengths. The second is the use of strengths; providing chances for a child to acknowledge and use their strengths. Research has suggested that when parents use strengths-based parenting their children are more likely to be mentally tough.

As parents, it is easy to see our children in a positive light and see them as having strengths in many areas. Developing a realistic and full understanding of a child's strengths and weaknesses may be tricky. It involves some reflection, which of course we have already highlighted as a key process in relation to our own mental toughness. It is also a key process when it comes to the mental toughness of our children. When we can identify our children's strengths, we can then begin to encourage our children to identify and use them. They can learn to choose tasks and strategies that maximise their chances of success, and in the process can further develop confidence and the willingness to face challenges.

Enabling positive childhood experiences

It is widely known that childhood experiences are important for children's development and that their impact extends well beyond childhood into adulthood. Popular terms in psychology and in education are positive childhood experiences and adverse childhood experiences. Positive experiences refer to things like healthy relationships with parents and peers, and positive experiences at school. Adverse childhood experiences are those that have the potential to cause harm to a child, either directly (e.g., abuse and neglect), or indirectly (e.g., through parental conflict, or family mental illness). Positive childhood experiences and adverse childhood experiences are separate, not at opposite ends of a spectrum, although of course their impacts are related, for example, positive experiences can attenuate the impact of adverse experiences.

Research has shown that people who report having positive childhood experiences also have higher levels of mental toughness (as well as higher levels of well-being). Therefore, as a parent, we need to ensure these positive experiences. Some of these we have an obvious role in, such as healthy relationships with parents; supportive behaviours and positive interactions, with a level of control should facilitate these relationships. Other experiences, such as healthy relationships with peers and positive experiences at school may seem more out of our control.

Although, as mentioned above, we need to allow children opportunities for experiential learning, and therefore need to allow them some autonomy, we can try and maintain some oversight over peer interactions and experiences at school. This just involves good communication and parental involvement in children's education. We can discuss, in a supportive manner, who our children have been spending time with and what they have been doing, and we ask children how things are going at school, attend parent's events, and raise any concerns with teachers.

Remembering domain specificity

Some scientific research has suggested that at least some components of mental toughness may operate in a domain-specific manner. This might mean, for example, that a child may be confident in their abilities at school, but not as confident in their abilities when taking part in sports, or they may have a high degree of risk orientation in terms of taking part in exciting activities like canoeing or paddle boarding, but not be as open and comfortable with trying something new in an educational setting, such as talking in front of a group. We may even see differences within a single domain.

For example, we know that children's attitudes and motivation at school may differ across different subjects. As parents, we, therefore, need to create the right environment and support to cultivate the development of mental toughness across all domains of a child's life. We should think about exposing our children to new situations, providing praise to improve their confidence, and encouraging them to reflect upon aspects of mental toughness across their school, home, and interpersonal lives.

Some insights from education

Research that has sought to develop our understanding of mental toughness has taken place in several domains. As mentioned earlier in the book, the concept of mental toughness was first developed and applied in sports. There is extensive literature on the role of coaches and others in developing an athlete's mental toughness. More recently, mental toughness has been explored in educational domains. It has been shown to be a useful predictor of educational outcomes and experiences. Research within an educational context has also generated some suggestions about how to help children develop mental toughness. These suggestions are presented in the table below for each of the mental toughness components.

Life control	Feelings of control are facilitated by supportive parenting and school involvement (i.e., taking an active role/interest in a child's education).
Emotional control	It is important to provide children with techniques and methods to control their emotions in difficult situations, for example, deep breathing exercises for dealing with exam anxiety.
Goal orientation	It is important to have a focus to encourage commitment (e.g., aiming for a particular grade).
Achievement orientation	Children are more likely to work towards goals if they set these goals themselves.
Risk orientation	Children are more like to take on challenges if parents/ teachers explain these challenges thoroughly.
Learning orientation	The extent to which children are willing to take on a challenge is linked to their past experiences of success (so encourage reflection).
Confidence in abilities	Confidence is boosted by frequent feedback from parents, teachers, and peers. It is particularly helpful if children can attribute this feedback to their own efforts.
Interpersonal confidence	Interpersonal confidence does not just come from having friends. For example, having a large friendship group could undermine opportunities to develop confidence in meeting new people. Children should be allowed opportunities to meet new people in different contexts.

Table 4 Developing mental toughness

14 DEVELOPING MENTAL TOUGHNESS TOOLKIT

Maria Lawless and Toni Molyneux

The mental toughness model provides a very useful framework to point the way forward and to help parents, guardians and teachers understand where a child might benefit from additional attention and support. In this chapter, we present a toolkit of practical activities that can be used to develop mental toughness and self-awareness in children.

All interventions and activities work to develop mental toughness, but they don't all work for everyone. Allow for some exploration and autonomy to find what your child enjoys and is most interested in. Remember that every child is different. They are individual.

Based on previous research, the toolkit activities are organised by six main intervention approaches; positive thinking, visualisation, anxiety control and relaxation, attentional control, goal setting and self-awareness via mental toughness questionnaires. More information on each of these approaches can be found in this chapter.

Support materials and worksheets for activities can be found at https://resilienthedgehog.com/#/resources.

For each activity, the mental toughness factor that it develops is identified. Although the mental toughness factors are independent – they each refer to (and measure) something separate, they are interrelated to some extent as they are all a component of this concept of mental toughness. Otherwise, all of the factors would be referring to the same thing. Therefore, you may find that an activity develops one particular factor of the mental toughness model but it may also have an unintended impact on another factor.

For example, you may choose activities to develop your child's confidence in their abilities but you may also inadvertently develop their risk orientation. As their confidence in their abilities grows, they may be more comfortable stepping outside of their comfort zone and trying new things. They possess more belief in themselves, in their knowledge and abilities to explore new things.

POSITIVE THINKING

The underlying principle of positive thinking is that we are what we think. We can think ourselves in or we can think ourselves out of action. It is about showing your child how to be optimistic.

There are three basic approaches to positive thinking – to train a person to think positively all of the time and to manage negative thoughts; to simply banish negative thoughts and get rid of them; to recognise that sometimes we a person can't avoid having negative thoughts, so how can we turn them into positive ones (reframing).

RANDOM ACTS OF KINDNESS

Kindness is best learned by feeling and experiencing it. A positive psychology activity – a random act of kindness is an action designed to offer kindness to others. This helps to develop positive thinking and build a sense of control.

The task is to carry out several random acts of kindness using the Random Act of Kindness (RAK) Bingo Card. You can either assign your child a random act to complete or allow them to pick their own.

Once they have carried out the act, they should take some time to reflect. Encourage them to think about the following:

1. How do they feel after they have completed a random act of kindness?
2. How do they think the recipient felt?

Encourage a discussion around positivity – that doing something for us helps the person doing and receiving the feel more optimistic. If possible, you should offer a small reward when all random acts have been completed – a sticker or a small treat maybe.

THINK THREE POSITIVES

Most people, when they encounter problems or setbacks dwell on them. In turn, this allows the problem to become significant, often out of proportion. This can dominate a person's mood or mindset. The reality is that we get most of what we do right, we just don't see it as special. And when we get things wrong, it feels like we get it all wrong. After a particularly bad day, it is easy to fall into the trap of focusing only on the bad things and it can be difficult to identify anything that might have been successful.

Focusing on the positives – big and small can, help to change a person's mood and therefore their mindset.

This is a positive thinking activity that helps to build confidence and develop a sense of control and achievement orientation. To complete this, you'll need the Think Three Positives Worksheet.

The Random Acts of Kindness worksheet should be completed at the end of each day.

1. Ask your child to think about what they have done today.
2. Using the dedicated space, they should write three things that they think or feel they have done well. It has to be something they have done and not something that has happened to them – like watching their favourite football team win. It doesn't have to be something big. It could be that they were well-mannered or they did something nice for someone.
3. They should reflect on how this makes them feel and record their thoughts. Encourage them to think about

how they feel about themselves if they have recorded an achievement they otherwise would have overlooked.

This activity should be completed regularly to help positive thinking become a habit.

Do this each day for a month and then take some time to reflect on all of the positive things your child has done or achieved. Once again, take some time to help them to reflect on how this makes them feel.

DRAW A PICTURE OF YOURSELF DOING SOMETHING YOU LOVE AND FEELING PROUD OF YOURSELF

Draw a picture of yourself when you are feeling good about yourself. It could be a moment of celebration like taking part in a dance or football competition. Draw a speech bubble and include phrases you would tell yourself. This activity will help children celebrate the small wins and provide confidence for other activities and areas of their lives.

1. Allow your child to draw a self-portrait of themselves using coloured pencils, crayons or markers.
2. The picture can include an environment or objects to help set the scene if they so wish e.g., football, dance studio etc.
3. Draw in a speech bubble.
4. Include statements that they felt in that moment e.g. I worked really hard to get into the football tournament, I am proud of myself etc.
5. When your child is finished with the drawing and writing check if anything is missing or anything else they would like to say to themselves. This can be helpful to recognise the small steps and positive talk that it can take to achieve a goal. You can add in observations that you make 'you trained consistently to get there' and 'there were times that you did not feel like going but you remained consistent.

DRAW A PICTURE OF YOURSELF WHEN YOU DO NOT FEEL YOUR BEST AND YOU MAY BE STRUGGLING WITH SOMETHING

Draw a picture of yourself when you are not feeling so good about yourself. It could be a moment of challenge, frustration, or an obstacle in your life. Draw a speech bubble and include phrases you would tell yourself. This activity will help children to externalise the challenges they feel. It will create an awareness of how we speak to ourselves when facing challenges. Awareness of our negative self-talk can lead us to be able to challenge whether the words we use are true or untrue and helpful or unhelpful.

1. Allow your child to draw a self-portrait of themselves using coloured pencils, crayons or markers.
2. The picture can include an environment or objects to help set the scene if they so wish e.g., any obstacle or challenge that may be causing them difficulty at a given time.
3. Draw in a speech bubble.
4. Include statements that they felt at that moment e.g. I really wanted to get on the football tournament but I am not good enough, nothing ever goes my way etc.
5. When your child is finished with the drawing and writing check if anything is missing or anything else they would like to say to themselves. This can be helpful to recognise their frustrations and negative talk can occur when we don't get something we want. It can give you as a parent a good insight into their mindset and whether they are in a 'fixed' or 'growth' mindset. You can add in observations that you make 'you said nothing ever goes my way' in your other picture you achieved something you wanted. Reflecting on what the child says can be helpful 'You feel like nothing ever goes your way'. Can we talk about this? I wonder why you think this?

It is important to allow children the space to feel disappointment and frustration and have an open discussion about it. Pictures can be used as a comparison to compare and contrast. This is not intended to make children feel better about frustrations but to create awareness, have a discussion and use their skills and confidence gained in other areas to find a way to overcome obstacles.

Dr. Dan Siegel discusses the 'Name it to tame it' theory which applies here. When we name feelings, obstacles and frustrations then we can tame them. If we keep this inside then we are unable to tame them.

MAKING AFFIRMATIONS

Positive affirmations are statements or phrases that when repeated can help to change negative thoughts and change behaviour patterns.

This is a positive thinking activity that helps to develop confidence and risk orientation.

For this, you'll need a blank sheet of paper.

1. Your child should draw a line down the centre of the paper.
2. On the left side of the sheet, they should write down five things they think they are good at.
3. On the right side of the sheet, they should write down five things that they think they are not so good at.
4. Ask them which list they think was easier to do. We find it easier to think about our weaknesses than our strengths which can hold us back. We are what we think! You have an amazing power over yourself because everything you know, do or feel is based on what is inside your mind. If we think negative or demeaning thoughts, these affect what

we do. These are called self-limiting beliefs and they can build up!

A way of dealing with self-limited beliefs is to develop positive affirmations. These are positive slogans that we adopt and keep in mind to help us to feel more positive.

5. Next, they should turn over the sheet of paper and write short statements – positive affirmations that they can hold in their mind and use every time they feel scared, nervous, or anxious or when they are doing something challenging. Why not turn this into an arts and crafts activity and have them create a post for each of their statements which can be displayed around the home?

Sample affirmations include:
- I can make a difference.
- I can achieve difficult tasks.
- If I work hard, I can achieve things.
- I enjoy solving problems.
- Achieving things makes me feel good and happy.
- I am going to learn from everything I do – even if it's challenging.
- I am going to enjoy learning new things.

SOMETHING YOU DIDN'T KNOW ABOUT ME

A simple activity that requires your child to identify something interesting about themselves and to share it. This is an activity that builds mental toughness across all four Cs but especially the confidence factor. They will be required to present their fact and talk about what it means to them – helping to develop confidence in abilities through reflecting on themselves and interpersonal confidence skills through talking about themselves and promoting their skills, knowledge and interests.

1. Ask your child to identify something about themselves that is interesting. It can be something they do, something they are good at or have done in the past or someone interesting or famous they have met. Or, it can be something they plan to do.
2. The task is for them to share their interesting fact with you and their family. Ask them to present their interesting fact, what exactly makes it interesting and how it makes them feel.
3. Afterwards, ask them to reflect on how it felt to present their fact. Did they find it easy or hard? Did they enjoy presenting to others and talking about themselves? Did they find any aspect of this difficult?

RAINBOW CHECK-IN

Even as adults the question, "How are you feeling today?" can make us feel overwhelmed. It's quite a vague question and it can be difficult to know where to begin when answering. Especially after a particularly difficult day. So, imagine how a child might feel when asked that same question. As parents, we want to know how our children are feeling, how their day has been or if something has made them feel happy or sad. But for a child, it is difficult for them to identify those different emotions, to process and understand those feelings to verbalise them and to connect them with different situations.

The rainbow check-in is a great activity for checking in on how your child is feeling and coping, and getting an accurate picture! It is a positive thinking activity that develops emotional control; helping your child to understand and manage their emotions. It also develops their sense of learning orientation through learning reflection skills.

For this activity, you will need to Rainbow Check-In sheet.

1. Invite your child to reflect on their day or their week.
2. Ask them to think about what their sunny spot was for the day or the week. Something that made them feel happy, joyful or proud. It might have been the best part of their day or week! Or maybe they were kind to themselves.
3. Did they have any rainy moments? Moments that made them feel down, disappointed or uncomfortable. Or maybe something might have challenged them or that they found difficult.
4. What was the rainbow moment of their day or their week? This might be something that brought them unexpected joy or happiness. Maybe it was something that made them smile or laugh unexpectedly. It could be something that they are looking forward to.

Make a note of these in the dedicated space on the Rainbow Check-In worksheet.

Afterwards, you should have a discussion with your child about what they have recorded. Talk to them about their experiences and emotions. Particularly those rainy moments they have identified. Think about what this might mean for them. Is there anything they can do to help if a similar situation arises? For example, if it was a situation that made them feel nervous or anxious the next time the situation arises, they could focus on their breathing (activities for this are outlined in the anxiety control section).

EMBODIMENT EXERCISE

This exercise is good for parents and children. It is a form of checking in with ourselves for adults and children. This is regularly used in art therapy.

1. Get an A4 sheet of paper and a coloured pencil.
2. Ask your child to draw the figure 8 on the A4 sheet. Set a

timer for three minutes and continue to loop around the figure eight until the three minutes are up.
3. There is no right or wrong way so reassure your child that they don't need to focus on having the perfect '8'.
4. When the time is up, have a look at the figure 8. Most of the time the top or bottom of the figure 8 will be bigger than the other.

If the top half of the figure eight is bigger this represents that you are more 'in your head' than your body. If the bottom half of the figure eight is bigger, this means you are more 'in your body' than in your head. Both have their place at different times. The awareness of where we are can show us how to balance ourselves a little more. If you are more in your head at a given time then grounding exercises can help you to feel more embodied. Putting your bare feet on the grass for five minutes has amazing grounding benefits. Walking, exercising or dancing can also put you more in touch with your body. If you are more in your body at a given time, you could listen to a podcast, read or do an activity that requires the mind to focus.

VISUALISATION

The underlying principle here is we can imagine success or we can imagine failure and we can learn from either. The challenge is to use visualisation more positively and productively. Visualisation is an extremely powerful way of learning to deal with stressful and anxiety-inducing situations.

VISUAL IMAGERY ACTIVITY

We will first begin with introducing the notion of visualising through demonstration. This will help your child to develop the skills needed to create mental images – learning to focus on the things we hear, see and feel.

1. Your child should close their eyes whilst you describe to them the things they would see whilst walking through a forest.
2. Describe what you would hear; birds, crunching branches under your feet.
3. Describe what you would feel; the warm breeze and the sun on your face as it beams through gaps in the branches.
4. Describe what you see; the trees high in the sky.
5. Invite your child to draw what you have described.

You can repeat this activity, choosing different scenarios and settings. This is the first step in learning to visualise. Learning and developing this skill can build mental toughness across all 4Cs. They will feel more in control of their lives and what happens to them as visualisation allows for a mental run-through of situations. It allows you to anticipate emotions and manage them in the situation. It can help them to imagine goals or targets for themselves – to see what they look like and therefore help them with achieving such goals or tasks. They will feel more comfortable trying new things if they can see it and prepare mentally beforehand. They will do all of this with more confidence in their skills and knowledge and will be better prepared to assert themselves and speak up.

VISUALISATION THROUGH READING

Another way of encouraging and developing the notion of visualising is through reading and learning to actively read.

As with the activity above, this activity will develop all factors of the mental toughness model.

For this, you'll need to select a descriptive book to read with your child. The Resilient Hedgehog books are a great tool for this (but hold off on showing the illustrations until after the activity).

1. Read the chosen book to your child, helping them to focus on the nouns, verbs, adverbs and adjectives. This will aid in honing in on the skills needed to create mental images and identify key information.
2. Invite your child to draw what they see in their minds as you read to them.
3. Afterwards, you can show them the book illustrations. Their depictions might look very different from the book but you can use this as an opportunity for discussion. If their depictions are different, why do they think this might be?

This activity should be repeated regularly.

WHAT WILL THE WORLD LOOK LIKE IN 20 YEARS?

An activity that will encourage your child to explore and visualise what the world might look like in 20 years' time. Encourage your child to consider a range of different scenarios, both positive and negative.

The goal here is to demonstrate how to use thoughts to focus on opportunities and learn how to deal with challenges and adversity. This visualisation activity develops life control and interpersonal confidence (sharing their ideas and feelings about their visualisation).

1. Invite your child to imagine what the world will look like in 20 years.
2. Focusing on one aspect of what they imagine, encourage them to think about what this might mean for them. How will they feel? What skills or resources might they need?
3. They should write down their ideas or draw a picture of what they visualise.
4. The next step in the task will be to present and share those ideas with you to build their interpersonal confidence skills.

Alternatively, make the activity craftier using the option below.

1. Invite your child to imagine what the world will look like in 20 years.
2. Focusing on one aspect of what they imagine, encourage them to think about what this might mean for them. How will they feel? What skills or resources might they need?
3. Give them an empty shoe box and allow them to create a 3D diorama or their visualisation. They can include recycling and arts and crafts materials to bring their visualisation to life. Children are naturally very good at this and an empty toilet roll tube could be used to represent a rocket, bed, or anything or their choosing.
4. The next step in the task will be to present and share those ideas with you to build their interpersonal

confidence skills.

ANXIETY CONTROL AND RELAXATION

Anxiety control and relaxation exercises involve looking at the physical costs of stress and focusing on the idea that psychological responses such as fear and worry have physiological consequences. For example, an increase in the stress hormone adrenaline has several consequences. It can increase breathing rate, make the heart beat faster and cause feelings of jitteriness and nervousness. Research shows that if you can bring these physiological responses under control, you can reverse those processes and learn how to deal with stressful and high-pressure situations.

We all experience these emotions at times but during those moments it can be difficult to get things under control – to think rationally. This is even harder for a child who cannot understand or regulate their emotions well. It's important during these situations to take time out. Time to breathe, to calm down, to process what is happening with the body and allow those physiological responses to come under control too.

PROGRESSIVE MUSCULAR RELAXATION

This activity shows you a way of releasing tension. When we feel anxious or frustrated, the body reacts by tightening muscles. Bringing this under control helps to release that built-up tension.

Progressive muscular relaxation is an anxiety control activity that, when done regularly can help us to better manage our emotions and the physical responses that come with emotions such as stress, worry, frustration and fear.

Create a relaxing environment for your child, ensuring they are sitting comfortably. Read through the steps below slowly to guide them through progressively relaxing their muscles.

At each step, the muscle should be tensed slowly and relaxed in between each step. Use the steps below to guide you through the activity, counting down the seconds at each step.

1. Make a fist with your right hand, tensing and holding for five seconds.
2. Relax the muscle for 10 seconds.
3. Bring your right forearm up to your shoulder and tense for five seconds – like you're 'making a muscle' to show how strong you are.
4. Relax the muscle for 10 seconds.
5. Bring your left forearm up to your shoulder as you did in the previous steps and hold for five seconds.
6. Relax the muscle for 10 seconds.
7. Raise your eyebrows as high as they will go as if you're surprised. Hold this for five seconds.
8. Relax the muscle for 10 seconds.
9. Open your mouth as wide as you can like you're yawning. Hold this for five seconds.
10. Relax the muscle for 10 seconds.
11. Now for your neck muscles – be careful as you tense. Face forward and pull your head back slowly, as though you're looking up to the sky.
12. Relax the muscles for 10 seconds.
13. To tense the muscles in your shoulders, bring your shoulders up towards your ears and hold for five seconds.
14. Relax the muscle for 10 seconds.
15. For your shoulder blades and back, push your shoulder blades back, trying to almost touch them together so that your chest is pushed forward. Hold this for five seconds.
16. Relax the muscle for 10 seconds.
17. Breathe deeply, filling your lungs and chest with air. Hold for five seconds.
18. Relax the muscles for 10 seconds.
19. Slowly tense your right thigh and hold for five seconds.

20. Relax the muscle for 10 seconds.
21. Slowly pull or point the toes of your right foot towards you to stretch your calf muscle. Hold for five seconds.
22. Relax the muscle for 10 seconds.
23. Now, point your toes away from you curling them down. Hold for five seconds.
24. Relax the muscle for 10 seconds.
25. Slowly tense your left thigh and hold for five seconds.
26. Relax the muscle for 10 seconds.
27. Slowly pull or point the toes on your left foot towards you to stretch your calf muscle. Hold for five seconds.
28. Relax the muscle for 10 seconds.
29. Now, point your toes away from you curling them down. Hold for five seconds.
30. And relax!

Afterwards, encourage your child to reflect on how they feel. Do they feel more relaxed and calmer? This activity should be done regularly to encourage a habit to develop. Then at times when your child might be feeling frustrated, angry, overwhelmed or anxious for example, they can take time out to help them to relax and calm down. To help to bring their emotions under control.

CONTROLLED BREATHING

One of the body's responses to fear, anxiety, and stress is muscle tension and disrupted breathing – a fight or flight response.

Controlled breathing is especially important. Most people only use 20% of their breathing capacity. By learning to breathe properly, a person can begin to feel less fatigued, less overwhelmed and more able to cope with their emotions and new challenges. They will also become more optimistic as they learn to cope better. Controlled breathing activities fall into the category of anxiety control. These help to develop emotional control, life control, risk orientation and confidence.

Controlled breathing is bigger, stronger, deeper and more rhythmic than typical shallow breaths. When done properly, it can help to relieve anxiety and improve circulation, concentration and digestion.

Below are some breathing activities you can use with your child.

BUBBLE ACTIVITY

Using bubbles to control and regulate children's breathing is an excellent technique. This can be used with children from a very young age to adults. Blowing bubbles is a universally playful experience. When children are anxious or stressed and may not feel calm enough for a conversation blowing bubbles will help them to relax and have fun.

1. Have a container of bubbles; these come in all different sizes. All work well and will help to settle the child through breathing. The bigger containers will require bigger breaths and this will calm a child quicker.
2. Blow the bubbles. Children can burst the bubbles which many will do naturally.
3. You can play around with this and ask the child to blow as many bubbles as they can.
4. You can then change it to blow as big a bubble as you can. This will lead to more focused intentional breathing.

WINDMILL ACTIVITY

Using a windmill toy to control and regulate children's breathing works well for children. They are active agents in controlling the pace, speed and strength of the breath. How they use their breath will influence how the windmill moves. Often at times when we are stressed, we tend to hold our breath. This is true for adults and children alike.

Connecting through play can help calm the child. Once we are connected and relaxed then we can have discussions. When a child is stressed or in 'fight or flight' mode there is no point in trying to begin with a conversation about what is wrong as the reasoning part of the brain is not in reach when distressed. Helping to calm them will provide benefits to everyone in the situation. With play, there is no right or wrong way so these steps are a guideline. Once the child is using breathing techniques they will return to a state of calm.

1. Get a toy windmill.
2. Blow on the windmill.
3. You can play around with this and ask the child to blow the windmill as fast as they can.
4. You can then change it to blow as slowly as they can. This will lead to more focused intentional breathing.
5. They can blow as hard as they can. You could link stories and get them to pretend they are the big bad wolf in the story of the three little pigs and get them to huff and puff as hard as they can. You could extend the activity by the adult taking the role of the three little pigs and playing it out with them).

DEALING WITH WORRIES

Worries are a normal part of life. Everyone experiences these at some time. Containment is used regularly in play therapy where the therapist holds a safe space and contains worries for a child through the therapeutic relationship. Worries can become crippling for children. Therefore, it is important that adults can help children look at and work through worries and also contain them and put them away at other times. This can help support emotional control and nightmares are one example of a situation where this can be helpful. This activity can be done in a few ways. Children can collect stones and paint a picture or a word that represents their worry (depending on their age). Alternatively, children can use Play-Doh or clay to represent their worries.

1. Allow your child to represent their worries through Play-Doh, clay or stones.
2. Allow the child to choose from different sizes of stones if they are using stones. If they are using Play-Doh or clay ensure they have a decent amount to play with and create.
3. The size of their worries will be different and children will naturally use bigger stones for bigger worries. Creatively they will use more Play-Doh or clay for whichever worry is causing them the most distress.
4. This will provide important feedback to the adult as to which worry is causing the most concern at a given time.
5. Containing the worries is an important part here. The process of creating and getting their worries out onto the 3D objects of stones, Play-Doh or clay will help the child process their worries. This will lead to talk and discussion about the worries. Adults may gain new insights at this stage.
6. Lunch boxes provide good containers and when there has been a sharing of worries, the containment part of the process begins. Again, a selection of sizes and choices for the child is an important part of the process. Allow the child to place their worries into the container. Affirm to the child that worrying is normal but you will put them away for today and you can look at them together when the child needs them.
7. Worries need to rest and go to sleep also.

MINDFULNESS BREATHING CARDS

Another way of helping to bring breathing under control is through the use of mindfulness breathing cards. A range of picture cards (e.g., rainbows, stars, butterflies, trees and bugs) are available to download.

Each card contains arrows and instructions for when to breathe in and out – the child simply traces the card with their finger as they follow the instructions.

CALMING GLITTER JAR

A glitter jar is a sensory tool. When shaken up, the swirling patterns of the glitter as it moves to settle at the bottom of the jar can help to calm emotions when a child is feeling overwhelmed.

They encourage a child to take some time to pause and calm down when they might be feeling angry, sad, stressed or emotional. Taking that time out can help them understand what is happening in their body and with their feelings and help them to feel refocused.

This is an arts and crafts activity that requires a jar with a lid, 60ml of glitter glue, 60g of glitter and a jug of hot water. A plastic jar rather than a glass jar is always a safer option to prevent any accidents.

1. Invite your child to pour some glitter glue into the jar. For larger jars, add more glitter.
2. Pour in some hot water and stir (do not use boiling water as the jar may break). This should be done by an adult to prevent any injuries.
3. When the lid is firmly in place, your child can shake the jar and watch the glitter calm and settle at the bottom.

ATTENTIONAL CONTROL

Attentional control exercises are about effective focus, sustained attention and concentration, enabling a person to work better and for longer. This is helping people to deal with interruptions and refocus their attention after a distraction.

Improving attentional control can produce a big boost to productivity, learning and well-being. This is a particular concern – with technology, we have a constant stream of information and distractions competing for our attention. How do we filter out the appropriate information and block out distractions to stay focused?

CONCENTRATION ACTIVITY

For this activity, you'll need the attentional control activity worksheets. There are a range of designs and patterns available to suit the interests of your child.

The task is to use a pen to trace the lines on the image – doing their best to keep focused and not stray off the lines.

This activity should be completed regularly. Each time their concentration and focus should improve – becoming more accurate and quicker at tracing the lines without getting distracted along the way.

US BASKETBALL ACTIVITY

A form of pressure training used before a sports game to enhance concentration and to remember how to stay focused. This is an attentional control activity that develops life and emotional control as well as learning orientation (through reflection) and confidence.

This activity should be carried out in pairs.

1. Facing your partner, stand with your hands behind your back. First, you will learn how to play the game and then you can play competitively.
2. Bring your hands up in front of you at chest height with your palms facing away from you. Your hands should be comfortably in sight.
3. Repeat this action a few times and try to get faster with each go.
4. Now time for the competition. This time, when you bring your hands up to your front, you need to decide on the number of fingers and thumbs to hold up. For example, you may decide to hold up 7 fingers whilst your opponent may hold up 4.
5. The winner is the person who counts all of the fingers and thumbs (so that's both people) and calls out the correct answer the fastest. In the example above, the winner would be the first person to call out 11.
6. Repeat this for four more rounds – starting with a reset with your hands behind your backs and counting down from three and signalling go.
7. In the last round, the slate should be wiped clean and it is winner-takes-all all!

When the game is over, encourage reflection. You can ask the following questions to help with this:

- How did they feel when the rules changed?
- What did they try to do to improve?
- How did they improve their concentration as the rounds went on?
- Did they become more determined to win with each round?
- How did they feel when the rules changed? For some people, this can throw them.

GOAL SETTING

The underlying principle of goal setting is that having goals and setting goals, even small goals give meaning and direction as well as fuel energy to achieve those targets and approach new challenges. This is particularly important when we look at the commitment and challenge scales. It is widely believed that goal setting provides a sense of purpose.

HEROES AND HEROINES

Using role models to overcome fears, concerns and disadvantages.

This is a positive thinking activity that develops challenge-risk and learning orientation as well as goal setting and confidence. Reflecting on and learning from others' experiences and their journey to their achievements (learning orientation) can help someone to feel more comfortable stepping outside of their comfort zone and trying new things (risk orientation) and to do so more confidently.

1. Ask your child to identify someone who they admire or look up to. This can be someone they know, or it can be someone famous.
2. They should create a poster about their chosen person – draw a portrait of them in the centre and surround the portrait with facts about that person
    a. They should think about what it is that they admire about them.
    b. What have they done or achieved?
    c. What do they think about their attitude – are they positive, do they work hard?
    d. They should think about things they might have overcome in the past and what they have achieved.
    e. Ask them to think about what they learned from this

person's experiences. For example, to not give up when things are hard. Encourage them to reflect on how this makes them feel.

TARGET PRACTICE

This is an exercise in goal setting. Setting realistic goals means that there is a reduced risk of disappointment or feelings of failure. Equally, goals shouldn't be easy. This can impact positive thinking which in turn impacts control, commitment and confidence.

For this activity, you'll need a waste paper bin and five small balls.

1. Position the waste paper bin somewhere safe and mark out a spot a few meters away.
2. Each person will have the chance to throw five balls into the paper bin. One successful ball in the bin equals one point.
3. Before starting, they should set a target of how many balls they can throw in the bin.
4. When you are ready to begin, invite them to stand on the spot you marked out. They have five shots.

Take some time for reflection. Encourage your child to think about their score. Were they more successful than they expected or did they score less than they anticipated? How did that make them feel?

Now it is time to reset before repeating the activity again. Encourage your child to reflect on the first round and set a new target based on their experience. When you are ready, repeat the exercise with another five shots.

Again, take some time to encourage reflection. How was their second attempt? Did they perform better this time? Were they closer to their target than in the previous round?

Setting goals too high or too low can result in disappointment, even if their score is okay.

SELF-AWARENESS AND THE MENTAL TOUGHNESS QUESTIONNAIRES

Self-awareness is a development activity in its own right. As highlighted in chapter two, as a parent, it is crucially important to be aware of your own behaviour and mindset and how those influence and impact the children in your care. Through the use of the Mental Toughness Questionnaire, the MTQPlus, we can increase our self-awareness and gain an understanding of why we respond to events the way we do. The MTQPlus is a 63-item psychometric that measures your mental toughness across the eight factors we have discussed throughout this book. This tool can be used to broaden your awareness of your behaviour and mindset. For more information, visit www.aqrinternational.co.uk.

15 DEVELOPING A CHILD'S MENTAL TOUGHNESS THROUGH BOOKS

Dorien van 't Ende

One of the great joys of parenting is reading books with your child. As a parent, it is a wonderful thing to see your child immersed in magical worlds and faraway lands. Reading books together can be a bonding experience that can start from day one.

Reading is in itself a fun activity, and there are many benefits to reading – boosting imagination, developing vocabulary, learning about emotions and interacting with others' emotions, to name but a few.

Research in 2021 found that when a six-year-old enjoyed learning, this continued well into adolescence and led to better attainment (Morris, 2021).

Other studies show that young children relate easily and quickly to stories that use animals as metaphors for humans rather than humans. It is thought that this makes a story safer for a child. Interestingly most are able to accept events and things that happen to the characters in the story and still seem to be able to relate to them.

For example, the idea of a hedgehog losing a favourite toy seems to be well understood and accepted by a young child. They can relate a time when they have lost something to the description in the story.

It may not come as a surprise that stories and books can also be useful in developing important life skills and personal qualities such as mental toughness in children... if we can engage them correctly.

Resilient Hedgehog, a division of AQR International, has developed a series of children's books that do just this (https://resilienthedgehog.com).

The books, aimed at ages 3 to 8, are beautifully illustrated stories that combine the joy of reading with the development of mental toughness through self-awareness. Each book focuses on one or more of the eight factors of mental toughness. Throughout the story, useful prompts are given to stimulate a discussion with a child.

The general approach to encourage a discussion is to talk about what they think is happening in each verse. What do they think is happening to the central character and what do they think of their reaction? Were there others involved? Were they helping or hindering? What is it that ultimately helps the central character to succeed?

Questions are provided to link the story to the child's life. Does anything like this ever happen to you or your friends? Finally, discuss what the point of the story is and how they can adopt the lesson in their lives and the situations they face.

In each book, the main character or characters face a difficult situation. Throughout the book, we find out how each character handles these challenges. In 'How the pelican got its name' we meet a group of pelicans with a very negative attitude to trying new things. They are so negative, they are called pelicants!

The pelicants refuse to dance because they may embarrass themselves. They won't play a game or sing songs. Going on a holiday is completely out of the question. All sorts of things could go wrong! Rather than focusing on positive outcomes, they are obsessed with negative results. Instead of taking the opportunity to learn from mistakes, they avoid the possibility of making a mistake altogether, because they don't want to be embarrassed. They just sit on their nest and watch other animals have fun and try new things.

It seems the pelicants have low levels of goal and risk orientation and they lack confidence in their own abilities. They never set themselves the goal of trying anything outside of their comfort zone for fear of failing.

Children are stimulated to relate the pelicants story to their own lives by discussing questions, such as 'What do you say 'no' to?' and 'What happens if you say 'no' all the time?'.

Later on in the story we meet two pelicants who are bored and fed up with never doing anything new.

When they receive an invitation to a party, the two pelicants decide to take a risk and go. This, again, links to risk orientation. They see this invitation as an opportunity rather than a threat. They think about all the positives that could happen: there could be cake, there may be music and dancing, maybe they will meet new friends!

Meanwhile, the other pelicants notice that their two friends have gone to a party and they decide they need to rescue them from a dangerous situation. Although their motivation is different, they, too, take a risk they would normally avoid. They go to a party, but not because they think it will be a positive experience. Instead, they go to make sure their friends are not in any trouble.

Children reading the book are asked to think about why the pelicants are going to the party and why the two pelicants are excited to go. Relating the story to their own life, children are asked, amongst other things, to tell about a time that they helped a friend

When the pelicants get to the party, they notice their friends are not in danger at all. Actually, it looks like they are having fun and they decide to join in. Do they look silly? Maybe a little bit, but they no longer care if they embarrass themselves. One of the pelicants concludes that they are always missing out on the fun, but it's better to look silly or try something new than not have a go at all. So, the pelicants decide that when they are faced with new opportunities, they are going to be brave.

Ultimately, the pelicants, who are now called pelicans, show that they have become more positive and resilient. A new situation is an opportunity because they have a sense of can-do and self-belief. They have the confidence that they can handle anything even if it does not go their way. Children are prompted to discuss if they ever tried something they were scared to do and how it made them feel.

How the pelican got its name and the other Resilient Hedgehog books are designed to take children on a journey where they actively think about what happens to the characters, as well as relate the story to their own life.

By thinking about, observing, and discussing the stories, the aim is to develop a child's positive attitude and resilience, so they feel confident to take on whatever life throws at them.

SUMMARY

The purpose of this book is to support parents, teachers, mentors and coaches etc. in understanding and developing mental toughness in children aged 2-8 years through exploring different dimensions of parenting.

Contributing authors were tasked with bringing their vast array of expertise and knowledge of early years development to facilitate the learning and growth of parents, teachers and the like.

Regardless of your background and knowledge, we hope that you have been encouraged to use this information, tools and techniques with the young people you care for.

To learn more about AQR International's work on Mental Toughness and the associated psychometric measures including MTQPlus highlighted in this book, visit www.aqrinternational.co.uk. To learn more about Resilient Hedgehog and it's offering of unique and innovative resources for parents and teachers, visit www.resilienthedgehog.com.

Finally, we wish you all the very best on your continued journey to raising thriving, resilient and positive young children.

REFERENCES

Baiocco, R., Cacioppo, M., Laghi, F., & Tafà, M. (2013). Factorial and construct validity of FACES IV among Italian adolescents. Journal of Child and Family Studies, 22, 962-970.

Clough, P. J., Earle, K., & Sewell, D. (2002). Mental toughness: The concept and its measurement. In I. Cockerill (Ed.), Solutions in sport psychology (pp. 32–43). London: Thomson.

Edmondson AC. 2004. Psychological safety, trust, and learning in organizations: a group-level lens. In Trust and Distrust in Organizations: Dilemmas and Approaches, ed. RM Kramer, KS Cook, pp. 239 –72. New York: Russell Sage

Hay, D. F., Payne, A., & Chadwick, A. (2004). Peer relations in childhood. Journal of child psychology and psychiatry, 45(1), 84-108.

La Greca, A. M., & Harrison, H. M. (2005). Adolescent peer relations, friendships, and romantic relationships: Do they predict social anxiety and depression. Journal of clinical child and adolescent psychology, 34(1), 49-61.

Landreth, G. L. (2023). Play therapy: The art of the relationship.

Perry, B. (2021). What Happened to You? Conversations on Trauma, Resilience and Healing.

Stosny, S. (2011) To feel better focus on what is more important. Psychology Today: Self-Regulation.

(Van der Kolk, B., 1994 'The Body Keeps the Score; Brain, Mind and Body in the Healing of Trauma)

Wiens, K. (2023). When Their Storm Meets Our Calm, Co-Regulation Occurs. Self-Reg 101. The MEHRIT Centre

EDITORS AND KEY AUTHORS

DOUG STRYCHARCZYK

Doug is the CEO of AQR International – Founded in 1989, AQR is now recognized, globally, as one of the most innovative developers of resources for individual, team and organizational development. AQR now works in 80+ countries.

In recent years, Doug has worked with Professor Peter Clough and Dr John Perry to define mental toughness and to create the world's leading measure of mental toughness.

Doug is now recognised as a leading authority on the application of mental toughness to the worlds of work, education, sport, health as well as social applications.

TONI MOLYNEUX MSc, BSc (Hons)

Toni is a Business Psychologist at AQR International. Toni holds a BSc (Hons) in Psychology from The University of Chester and an MSc in Organisational Psychology from Alliance Manchester Business School. She also holds British Psychological Society Level A and B qualifications in Occupational Test Use.

Toni coordinates and delivers large-scale projects within AQR's educational division. With a passion for social mobility, she works with local authorities to deliver programmes, including strategic school improvement-funded projects. She leads AQR's programmes with educational institutions to help improve the performance, well-being and employability of young people.

CONTRIBUTORS

NASREEN BASHRAHEEL

Nasreen holds a BA in HRM with Management and an MA in HRM. She is a Chartered MCIPD. She is working on a Doctorate in Transdisciplinary on work-based projects. Certified Team Coach Practitioner, ICF Professional Certified Coach (PCC), European Mentoring and Coaching Council Practitioner, Senior Certified Professional Coach, MTQ 48 & MTQ Plus Licensed User – Mental Toughness, Certified Business Psychologist, Culture Accredited Practitioner.

Over the years, Nasreen Bashraheel has displayed inclusive leadership coaching and mentoring in dealing with parents and caregivers of different backgrounds, languages, and perspectives by unleashing the power of resilience and promoting mental toughness.

Nasreen is a Mental Toughness coach, she collaborated in writing this book to make a positive difference and help parents, and caregivers improve their mental toughness, learn about resilience and have a positive mindset. Her main interest is to focus on the holistic development for both Sport Coaches and Athletes.

DORIEN VAN 'T ENDE

Dorien van 't Ende MA is the mother of Niamh Lotus and Polly Philou. She lives with her partner, Jonathan, and dog, Tobie, in Chester, Great Britain. Originally from the Netherlands, Dorien's keen interest is in early years development and helping parents to provide the best upbringing they can manage.

ANNA GOLAWSKI

Anna Golawski is a qualified coach and facilitator who works predominantly with leaders and managers in both the private and public sectors. She has over 20 years of experience working for large organisations and brings with her strong HR and commercial experience. Anna is a seasoned professional with extensive experience in driving diversity and inclusion (D&I) strategies within organisations and specialising in mental toughness and neuroleadership. She has contributed to other published books and articles on mental toughness and coaching.

OKTAWIA HRYP-CZERWIŃSKA

Oktawia Hryp-Czerwińska – by education - sociologist, master's degree in human resources management and business trainer. She has over 10 years of training experience in business with various industries. She is also a licensed MTQ consultant. Her main specialization is developing personal effectiveness and mental toughness. Constantly looking for connections and mutual influences between these two areas, she supports personal development by working individually and in groups. Working with different generations in business, she constantly observes how important mental toughness is in the context of personal effectiveness among different generations and after changes taking place in the labour market.

MARIA LAWLESS

Maria Lawless has a wide background of experience and qualifications in Ireland. Maria holds a BA (Hons) Degree in Psychology from Dublin Business School. Maria is a qualified primary school teacher with a Higher Postgraduate Diploma in Primary Education from Hibernia College. Maria holds a Certificate in Therapeutic Play Skills and a Diploma as a Play

Therapist from the National University of Galway and APAC. Maria is a member of Play Therapy Ireland (PTI).

Maria has spent many years teaching various class levels in the mainstream Irish education system in a DEIS band 1 school. Maria has spent five of these years working as a home school liaison teacher, working directly with parents to support and empower them to support their children in reaching their full potential. This role has a large focus on attendance, participation and retention with families who are finding these challenging. Working as a team with parents was key to identifying and overcoming the unique challenges that face their family including school refusal and working with external organisations to support the children and parents.

Maria job shares and teaches for half of the week for the Department of Education and provides play therapy privately with her 'Flawless Play Therapy' business to children facing adversities, challenges or trauma for the other half of the week in Dublin. Play and the therapeutic powers of play are an integral part of Maria's work.

HELEN ST CLAIR-THOMPSON

Helen is a Reader in Psychology at Newcastle University. She has several teaching and leadership responsibilities and has a broad range of research interests related to psychological constructs that can be applied in educational settings. She has published work evidencing the importance of mental toughness in school and university settings, and also work concerned with the role of childhood experiences in mental toughness. She is also a parent, which of course is particularly relevant given the topic of this book.

KASIA WIĘCKOWSKA

Kasia Więckowska - certified mental trainer, certified mental toughness consultant, Social Skills Trainer, Anger Management Trainer, soft skills coach, certified Crisis Consultant, solution-focused brief therapy practitioner. A brain and learning enthusiast. Additionally, possesses 20 years of experience gained in international organizations in change management and guiding people through changes. A specialist working with kids and teenagers. President of the Board of the Polish Foundation - Fundacja Dziecięce Skrzydła Mocy - developing mental toughness in kids, teens and young adults, helping young people to develop critical life skills to succeed in life.

About Resilient Hedgehog

Resilient Hedgehog is a publisher with a mission. That mission is to create unique materials and resources that help parents develop their children to be the best version of themselves that they can be.

Resilient Hedgehog is a division of AQR International, an organisation which is recognised as a thought leader on the Mental Toughness concept. Mental Toughness is increasingly recognised as one of the most important qualities about which a person can develop self-awareness. It embraces ideas such as mindset, resilience, optimism, positivity, grit and character.

Although all Resilient Hedgehog stories look like normal children's stories, each offers clear learning opportunities about an aspect of resilience and positivity. These cover key elements such as developing a sense of "can do", building confidence, having courage and making and keeping promises.

The Resilient Creatures series of books describes challenges and situations to which a child can relate using animals as metaphors. The books enable children to learn about the 8 factors that contribute to developing a resilient and positive mindset.

Books are written to be used in two ways:

- To be read by parents or teachers and explored with children (3 – 6 years).
- To be read by children (typically 6 years or older) and explored with parents.

About the Books

- The beautifully detailed illustrations encourage a child to explore what's happening in the story.
- Written in rhyming text perfect for reading aloud.
- Fun facts about the animal characters featured in each book.
- Hits and tips for discussion are shown throughout the story including extra characters and talking points.
- The website supports each story with downloadable resources for parents/teachers
www.resilienthedgehog.com.

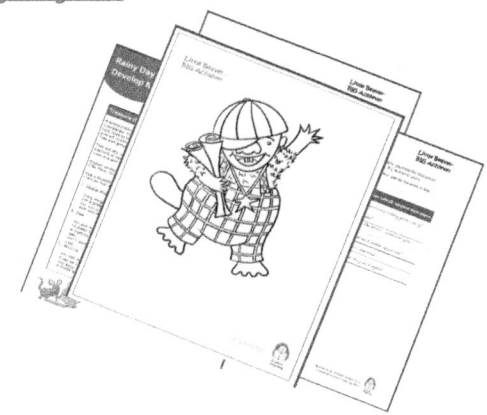